920
PFL   Pflaum, Rosalynd

          Marie Curie and
          her daughter
          Irène

DUE DATE	BRODART	05/94	21.50

Marie Curie

and Her Daughter
Irène

Marie Curie

BY
ROSALYND PFLAUM

and Her Daughter
Irène

LERNER PUBLICATIONS COMPANY · MINNEAPOLIS

The author would like to thank two people at the Institut du Radium in Paris who assisted enormously with this book. Mme Monique Bordry, the librarian at the Curie Pavilion, was patience personified, as was her colleague, M. Brunot, who furnished the photographs. Two others on this side of the Atlantic also provided invaluable help. Lois Fruen, who recently won the American Chemical Society's national award for excellence in high school chemistry teaching, read over the manuscript and furnished the two experiments in the back of the book. These flesh out identical ones Marie Curie gave to her students, including Irène, at the Cooperative. Susan Breckner Rose, the editor for this book, gave unstintingly of her time and efforts, over and above the call of duty.

Photographs courtesy of the Laboratoire Curie, Institut du Radium, Paris, with the exception of those on pages 18, 20, 21, courtesy of Seeberger/© Arch. Phot. Paris/S.P.A.D.E.M.

Library of Congress Cataloging-in-Publication Data

Pflaum, Rosalynd.
    Marie Curie and her daughter Irène / Rosalynd Pflaum.
        p.   cm.
    Includes bibliographical references and index.
    Summary: Presents the life stores of Marie Curie, discoverer of radium, polonium, and natural radiation, and her daughter Irène Joliot-Curie, discoverer of artificial radiation.
    ISBN 0-8225-4915-8
    1. Curie, Marie, 1867-1934—Juvenile literature. 2. Joliot-Curie, Irène, 1897-1956—Juvenile literature. 3. Chemists—Poland—Biography—Juvenile literature. 4. Physicists—France—Biography—Juvenile literature. [1. Curie, Marie, 1867-1934. 2. Joliot-Curie, Irène, 1897-1956. 3. Chemists. 4. Physicists.]
I. Title.
QD22.C8P45   1993
540'.92'2—dc20
[B]
                                              92-2453
                                                CIP
                                                 AC

Manufactured in the United States of America

1 2   3   4   5   6   98 97 96 95 94 93

Preface

When I was a girl growing up, I read Ève Curie's biography of her mother, *Madame Curie*. Writing shortly after her mother's death, Ève gave, for the first time, a detailed account of the fascinating lives of Marie and Pierre Curie.

As I got older and began to write the biographies of great French men and women, it was only a matter of time before the Curie family once more absorbed me. I discovered by great good luck that a friend knew the retired director of the Institut du Radium, Dr. Raymond Latarjet. This distinguished scientist proved to be my key to the Curies' world. Counseled by Mme Monique Bordry, the charming librarian at the Curie Pavilion and a fine science writer herself, I stepped into the recent past.

A few friends and colleagues of Marie and Pierre—and a good many more of Irène and Fred Joliot-Curie—were still alive when I began my research. Armed with a tape recorder, I hurried from rendezvous to rendezvous in the scientific and intellectual heart of Paris. Strangely enough, no one had ever thought of interviewing these people before. They, as well as the two Joliot children, who are distinguished scientists themselves, received me most courteously.

I hurried back to the Curie Pavilion to record my impressions and write up my notes. There Marie Curie's own office—subsequently Irène's and Fred's—had been placed at my disposal. Once a month a crew appeared, armed with Geiger counters, to test the radio-activity—which decreases by half every 1600 years—of the room and furniture and be sure it was safe for humans to be there.

Today, to better preserve this priceless heritage, no one is permitted to work in the director's office at the Curie. All the original documents, both at the Curie and at the Bibliothèque National, have been replaced by photocopies. Even so, the thrill of reliving some of the most exciting moments in the history of science in their original settings is inescapable. May some of those who learn of the incredible story of Marie Curie and her daughter Irène—two women who won three Nobels—be inspired to follow in their footsteps.

To Leo, who would know why

Contents

The photo of Professor Vladislav Sklodowski and his three daughters—Manya (Marie), Bronya, and Hela (left to right)—was taken in 1890, shortly before Manya went to Paris and while Bronya was home for a visit. Bronya, who had become a prize cook, was studying to be a doctor in Paris. Hela, the beauty of the family, had inherited her mother's beautiful voice and was taking lessons from Warsaw's finest singing teacher.

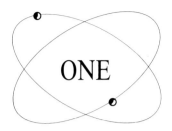

ONE

Manya Sklodowska

1867-1891

In mid-November 1903, a telegram transformed Marie and Pierre Curie's lives. The young couple received word from Stockholm, Sweden, that they and a colleague, Henri Becquerel, had been awarded the Nobel Prize for physics. Receiving the world's most famous scientific award catapulted the two researchers from celebrity status to international glory. Photographers and journalists took up their trail.

When the press descended on the Curies' home in Paris, Marie and Pierre were out. Only their daughter, Irène, and her Polish nurse were there. The reporters pestered the pair with questions. The nurse froze, then fled to the kitchen, pleading that she did not understand French. One reporter, undaunted, turned to Irène and asked where her parents were.

"At the laboratory, of course," the six-year-old replied self-assuredly. She stared hostilely at the intruders. How stupid! Where else would they be? She ignored any further questions and resumed playing with Dido, her black-and-white cat.

The following day, a picture of Irène and Dido made the front pages of the Paris newspapers—as did the conversation with the child and her nurse.

Marie Salomée Sklodowska was born on November 7, 1867, in the family's small upstairs apartment over a girls' boarding school on Freta Street in Warsaw's old quarter. Warsaw was in the part of Poland that, at the time, was occupied by Russia. An ash-blonde with gray eyes, Manya— as she was called—was the fourth daughter and fifth child of the school's director, Bronislawa Sklodowska. Manya's father, Vladislav Sklodowski, taught physics and mathematics in small secondary schools. Both Manya's parents came from poor families of the minor nobility. Shortly after Manya was born, her mother, in frail health, resigned from the Freta school and devoted herself to raising their large family.

By the time Manya was five, her mother had developed tuberculosis. Bronislawa Sklodowska was determined that

The Sklodowski children—(from left to right) *Zosia, Hela, Manya, Jozio, and Bronya—about 1870*

The pension Sikorska in Warsaw, where Manya was the youngest and brightest student in her class—about 1877

her family should not notice her suffering any more than she could help. Every Saturday night, she managed to sit with her brood, listening to Professor Sklodowski read aloud from the classics while she mended the children's clothes and made their boots with a small cobbler's awl and knife. At the rate the five children were growing, store-bought shoes were an unattainable luxury on a teacher's salary.

The Sklodowskis were patriotic to the core. Inevitably, as Russia tightened its control over Poland, Professor Sklodowski was dismissed from job after job on the grounds that he was not sufficiently pro-Russian. Police informers had infiltrated all walks of life. The Sklodowskis, in an attempt to make ends meet in their next apartment, were reduced to taking in boarding students. As the youngest Sklodowski, Manya slept rolled up in an animal skin on the sofa in the dining room. She had to be up at 6:00 A.M. so the table could be set for the boarders' breakfasts.

Unfortunately, these strangers did far worse than intrude on the family's privacy. They introduced the dreaded typhoid disease into the household. Soon two of Manya's older sisters were shaking and moaning with typhoid fever, and Zosia, the oldest, died. Two years later, tuberculosis finally claimed Manya's mother.

The linens may have been threadbare, the clothes patched, the meals sometimes skimpy, but food for thought was never lacking in Manya's home. Even after Bronislawa's death, reading together Saturday night remained the high spot of the week for the close-knit family.

Manya graduated from high school at age 16, amid the customary flourish of trumpets and speeches. On a summer afternoon so stifling that not even a cloud moved overhead, the Grand Master of Education placed around Manya's slender neck a multicolored ribbon with the coveted gold medal of number-one student dangling from it. The sun's rays kept bouncing off that glistening disk as Manya returned to the platform again and again. Soon she had an armful of books as prizes for excellence in mathematics, history, Russian literature, German, English, and French.

Instead of being able to enjoy her triumph, Manya fell sick. Professor Sklodowski wisely decided that Manya needed a prolonged rest, and he shipped her off to the country for a year to visit various relatives. Lancet, Manya's thoroughly spoiled, enormous brown pointer, accompanied her. With no manners, he jumped up affectionately on every-

A sketch Manya made of the frisky, energetic Lancet in her notebook

one. In winter, when Manya and her cousins participated in the *kulig,* Lancet bounded after their sleigh. During an enchanted weekend of carnival, the young group journeyed across the snowy landscape from house to house in a mad round of gaiety. No one danced a faster *mazurka* or a more enthusiastic *krakoviak* than Manya, the ribbons in her festival crown swirling round her blonde locks.

When Manya returned to Warsaw, she had not yet decided how she was going to earn a living, but her older sister Bronya was determined to become a doctor. This meant going abroad to study before settling down to practice in Warsaw. The universities in Geneva and Paris were the only two in Europe that admitted women to graduate work. The best way for Bronya to earn the money for her studies was by tutoring others. Manya decided to help her sister by tutoring also.

A friend of theirs persuaded Manya and Bronya to attend the illegal night school she was directing. Meeting four nights weekly, the school was called the "Floating University" because it had no permanent home and met in different garrets and cellars. There was no charge, but to participate required courage. Since it was a Polish school where only Polish was spoken, both teachers and students were subject to prison terms or possible deportation to Siberia if the Russian authorities found them out. The students were mostly young women for whom there was no other way to obtain further education.

Like the other students, Manya was filled with idealism. She too wanted to help free Poland from Russia. The director took for granted a woman's right to participate in this struggle. By completing the education of the Floating University's members, the director hoped to build up a corps of teachers who would educate the illiterate poor and thus, by a chain reaction, would liberate Poland. Anxious to do her share, Manya arranged to come twice weekly to a nearby dressmaker's workroom where she read to the seamstresses while they stitched.

After tutoring for over a year, Manya and Bronya still only managed to scrape together enough money to purchase a one-way train ticket to Paris and to cover Bronya's expenses for the first year of her five-year doctor's program. At that rate, Manya figured, it seemed like 20-year-old Bronya would be old and gray before she ever set foot in France. So Manya decided to hire herself out as a governess. Since she would get meals, lodging, and laundry free, most of her small salary could go to Bronya. Bronya could then go to Paris, and when she graduated, she in turn would help subsidize Manya's education abroad.

Manya's departure from Warsaw in 1886 was the beginning of a new life. After a three-hour train trip north, followed by a monotonous, five-hour sleigh ride across vast, treeless plains hushed beneath heavy snow, Manya reached the home of the Zorawski family. She was greeted warmly, especially by the two sisters who were to be her pupils. Consumed with curiosity, they could not take their eyes off their new governess in her plain, unadorned frock with her hair neatly arranged under a faded, hand-me-down hat.

The Zorawskis lived on a large farm in the heart of the sugar-beet region of Poland. Dinner-table conversation centered around gossip, sugar beets, and the damage caused by the latest frost. Manya missed her own family and their heated discussions over higher education for women and the rights of Russian-occupied Poland.

Manya was appalled at the wretched conditions of the peasants who lived in the hovels nearby and who worked in

Manya worked here, at the Zorawskis' house, from 1886 to 1889.

the sugar-beet fields and factory. In her free time, she set out to give the peasants' illiterate children two hours of school daily. The Zorawskis obligingly shut their eyes to such treasonable activity. Often the children's parents—dirty, smelly, and uneducated like their barefoot offspring—crowded in too, curious to see what Manya was up to.

Bronya was now in Paris and counting on the money her sister managed to send monthly. So Manya, homesick though she was, did not take any summer vacation. That summer she met Casimir, the oldest Zorawski son, who was home from the university in Warsaw on vacation. He was a most welcome link with sorely missed Warsaw. The two fell in love.

Unfortunately, while the Zorawskis thought the world of Manya as their children's governess, they saw her in a different light as a possible daughter-in-law. Casimir, who was studying to be an agricultural engineer, could never, as a Pole, receive a well-paid post upon graduation. He would need a rich wife to support him. Marriage with Manya was out of the question, and a crestfallen Casimir obediently returned to Warsaw.

This was Manya's first experience with love, and she was crushed. But her contract still had two years to go. The pay was steady, and Casimir was out of sight. So the practical young woman swallowed her pride and stayed on as if nothing had happened.

Time seemed to drag on like a jail sentence. Since her evenings were free, Manya read till late at night, furthering her education with books borrowed from the factory library. She turned more and more to science, which she considered a powerful tool to aid humanity. Impressed by her interest, a chemist at the sugar-beet factory gave her chemistry lessons. Although there was no place to do laboratory work, Manya decided that chemistry was what she wanted to study if she ever got to Paris. For by now Bronya no longer needed Manya's money. Bronya was getting married to a Polish doctor and wrote Manya to start saving for her own study in Paris.

When Manya returned to Warsaw in the spring of 1889, she had the thrill of conducting her first chemistry experiments. Up to that point she had only read about them. Almost every evening, she hurried to #66 Krakovsky Street, crossed a well-kept courtyard, and entered a tiny, one-story building at the far end. Above the door was engraved "Museum of Industry and Agriculture." This misleading name had been chosen by its founder, Manya's cousin, to disguise another of the city's clandestine academies. No Russian law prohibited teaching science to young Poles inside a museum. Here, after hours, Manya attempted practical experiments in the school's crude laboratory. A chemistry teacher and his aide gave Manya a course in chemistry in their free time. If her cousin was around, he would entertain her with tales about Dmitri Mendeleev—the legendary Russian chemist, whose assistant he had once been.

Bronya kept urging Manya to come west. Manya was troubled at leaving her frail, elderly father to go so far away, but she was comforted to know he was going to live with her brother Jozio, who was now married. If she felt guilty about her happiness at finally being able to study at the Sorbonne, or if she felt any sadness at leaving her beloved Poland, patriotism eased her conscience. In two or three years, she would return far better able to help her homeland than if she stayed at home. Although she had only a secondary high-school degree, Manya's ambitious sights were set on an advanced scientific education. This goal was extraordinary for a woman of that day, even more so for a Polish woman.

Gustave Eiffel built his famous tower as a centerpiece for the World's Fair of 1889, two years before Manya arrived in Paris.

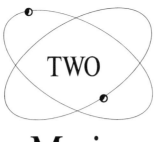

TWO

Marie

1891-1895

Shortly before her 24th birthday, Manya kissed her father good-bye and climbed up into the third-class compartment of the transcontinental steam train. Manya was equipped for the three-and-a-half days of travel with food and drink, books, and a blanket. She also carried a chair. She planned to switch to fourth-class when she crossed the Polish border, and those cars had only a bench around their sides and no seats.

Upon her arrival at the Gare du Nord in Paris, Manya took the next horse-drawn omnibus that came along. Climbing the little corkscrew stairs, she mounted to the top where the seats were cheapest because they were exposed to the wind and rain. They also had the best view. Eagerly Manya peered from side to side as the great, gray-dappled Percherons ambled along. The Eiffel Tower loomed even higher than she had expected. Electric lamps were being installed along the great boulevards that cut through Paris. The streets were crowded with the new three- and four-wheeled, internal-combustion vehicles that preceded the modern automobile.

The tiny second-floor flat of her sister and brother-in-law—Bronya and Casimir Dluski—overlooked the leafless trees of the outlying, working-class district of La Villette. Casimir's patients were the Polish émigrés and the butchers who worked in the neighboring slaughterhouses. Bronya, who was a gynecologist—a specialist in women's diseases —treated their wives.

Bronya had made the Dluskis' little flat comfortable with furniture picked up at auctions. She gave Manya a private room at the back. Polish books lined the shelves, Polish pictures adorned the walls, even the enticing aromas of Polish cooking filled the air. Only Polish was spoken here, and a samovar—for making tea—bubbled around-the-clock. To come to such familiar surroundings helped Manya adapt to life in a city and country so new to her.

Manya had allowed herself a couple of days to see Paris before classes started. She felt she was on a different planet. Browsing through the books at the numerous stalls along the *quais*, or landings, bordering the Seine, she no longer looked over her shoulder to see if she was being followed by the

Manya wandered along the Left Bank of the Seine, by the booksellers' stalls, when she first came to Paris—and had some time.

The Paris Opera House — about 1900

Russian police. She strolled through the Latin Quarter on the Left Bank, the heart of intellectual Europe. Paint-splattered artists, sitting at small zinc-covered tables, sipped demitasses — small cups of coffee — or glasses of wine while discussing openly, and heatedly, the paintings at the latest exhibits.

On November 3, 1891, Manya set out, her worn-leather portfolio under her arm, to sign up for fall classes at the Sorbonne, part of the Université de Paris. Using the French version of her name, "Marie" — as Manya would be called from this point on — she registered to prepare for a *licence ès sciences*, the degree that was the first step toward a doctorate.

Marie was prepared to find her background knowledge skimpy, but she was dismayed to discover how inadequate her understanding of mathematics was. The real shock was that her French was also inadequate. The tiered amphitheater where her lectures were held was poorly lit, so reading the great blackboard running along the back of the stage posed another problem. Marie was always one of the first to arrive in order to get a front-row seat as close as possible to the blackboard and the lecturing professor.

Although Marie had so much catching up to do, it was impossible to study at the Dluskis' in the evening. After working hard during the day, her brother-in-law wanted to relax at night. Members of the small Free Polish Colony were continually dropping in. Vodka and poppy-seed cakes, made each day by Bronya in some rare spare moment, appeared, and the little flat resounded with excited talk as the displaced Poles remade Poland and the world.

Marie soon decided the two hours spent daily, going to and fro, could be put to better use—over her books. Also, bus tickets were a drain on her shallow pocketbook. So in March, with a loan from the Dluskis to pay a man with a pushcart to transport her few possessions, Marie moved across the Seine to the Latin Quarter. Here students found cheap rents and food. Although she was very poor, Marie had as much money as many of her classmates. But instead of sharing a room, as most did, Marie deprived herself of all but the barest necessities for the luxury of living alone.

She moved frequently. Picking locations within a short walk of her classes and laboratories, Marie always chose the cheapest room—in the garret, with a single window that rarely shut properly. She never had less than six flights of stairs to climb. Because she was directly under the eaves, her room was broiling in summer and freezing in the winter. Generally she had cold tiles on the floor, and of course, Marie had no rug. She had only a small table, one kitchen chair, a washbowl and a pitcher for water, a coal scuttle, an oil lamp, and an iron folding-bed. Her mattress and bedding had come with her from Warsaw in an old trunk that doubled as a second chair. For water, she filled a jug from a tap on one of the lower landings. She bought coal by the lump from a dealer on a nearby street, but she only lit her small stove in the coldest weather. Kerosene for her one lamp, which she needed to read by, and alcohol for a tiny cooking heater about the size of a saucer rounded out her small list of necessities.

Since Marie knew virtually nothing about cooking and cared less, one saucepan was more than enough. She also had two plates—in case one broke—and three tumblers, a present from Bronya, so that when the Dluskis came to see her, Marie could offer them a glass of tea. Marie lived on tea, radishes, and buttered bread. On rare occasions, she treated herself to boiled eggs or stopped to sip a cup of hot chocolate in a nearby creamery.

On cold nights, Marie studied in the warm, gas-lit library of Sainte Geneviève. When the library closed at 10:00 P.M., she scurried home, broke the ice in her pitcher to get water to make some tea, and studied a little longer before jumping into bed with all her clothes on. To try to keep warm when the thermometer dropped lower still, she piled her coat and her one other dress, as well as her two towels and extra sheet, on top of herself. Often, near the end of the month, she would run out of coal. Then she had to shiver and shake, with hands reddened and swollen by the cold, until the first of the following month.

One day, during Marie's first spring in Paris, Bronya received an emergency call. Marie had fainted on the sidewalk in front of her apartment. The Dluskis both examined her when they picked her up and arrived at the same diagnosis: starvation. Her brother-in-law chided her. Bronya scolded. A beefsteak did wonders. With difficulty, the Dluskis kept Marie with them long enough to fatten her up a little. But she was too stimulated by and interested in what she was studying to stay long. Later she would claim: "This life, painful from certain points of view had, for all that, a real charm for me."

Because Marie was not sufficiently caught up with her class, she did not return to Warsaw for summer vacation. Instead she remained in sultry Paris to take extra mathematics courses and work on her French.

Marie's herculean efforts were not in vain. In July 1893, she received her coveted *licence ès sciences physiques*. She was not only the first woman to pass this test and get such a degree at the Sorbonne but, in a class of 30, the young Polish woman was number one.

Spending any remaining money on gifts, Marie set off on her first trip home. Professor Sklodowski felt consoled for her long absence by her academic success, but he was shocked at her pinched, tired expression when she stepped off the train. All summer long, he enjoyed fretting over her and restoring her health.

For Marie, ambition was slowly taking the place of family ties. She realized that a solid mathematics background was essential if she wanted to be fully qualified when she returned home for good. But the question of financing further work in Paris to obtain a second degree posed the same old problem: money. Fortunately, Marie received the Alexandrovitch Scholarship, which was given annually to assist one deserving Pole's study abroad. Fifteen more months in Paris were hers!

In the spring of 1894, Marie received a paid commission from the Society for the Encouragement of National Industry to do a study of the magnetic properties of different steels. She started the project working in the laboratory of one of her favorite teachers, but she soon found she needed more room. Marie did not know where to turn for assistance.

Meanwhile, a friend of Marie's from Warsaw came to Paris on her honeymoon. Her husband, a professor of physics, had been asked to give some lectures. He had recently met Pierre Curie, one of the most promising of the young French physicists. Curie was interested in basic research on magnetism and was also the laboratory chief at the newly founded School of Industrial Physics and Chemistry of the City of Paris—or EPCI, as it was called. The newlyweds thought that perhaps he might be able to help. They invited Marie to come to their boardinghouse for tea to meet Pierre.

Pierre Curie was a gentle, straightforward man who preferred to live his life as anonymously as possible in the ivory tower of science. His father would have preferred to devote his life to scientific research, but he had had to practice medicine in order to support his wife and two sons. Dr. Eugène Curie encouraged the boys' natural inclination for science and taught them how to observe facts and interpret them correctly from an early age.

Jacques, the older boy, readily adapted to a normal school life. Pierre—born in 1859, four years after his brother —did not. His parents were his first teachers. He was still very young when he was introduced to formal schooling with the beginning lectures for his doctorate in physics at the Sorbonne. Two years later, Pierre received his *licence ès sciences*. Because he had to earn his living, he was forced to postpone further work toward his Ph.D. Pierre accepted an

*Jacques and
Pierre Curie,
with their
parents—
Sophie-Claire
and Eugène
Curie in 1878*

appointment as laboratory chief at EPCI. What limited time
Pierre could call his own, he devoted to research.

Pierre was standing near the window when Marie entered her friends' sitting room. He looked younger than 35
—Marie was then 26—and was rather handsome. He was
tall and his clothes, which were cut on ample, old-fashioned
lines, hung loosely. Pierre's slow, reflective manner of speaking, his simplicity, and his grave smile inspired confidence in
Marie. It was her lack of a laboratory that brought Marie and

Pierre together, and unfortunately, this was the one thing he could not offer her. He did not even have a laboratory himself. In a system that put teaching before research, space posed a problem—indeed, even Pierre's workbench at EPCI was in a corridor running between the stairs and his classroom.

Marie and Pierre saw each other occasionally at meetings of the Physics Society. When his paper "On Symmetry in Physical Phenomena: Symmetry of an Electrical Field and of a Magnetic Field" appeared, Pierre sent Marie a copy of it with a scribbled personal dedication. Nothing could have pleased Marie more. For Pierre personified her ideal of a successful scientist. Equally important in Marie's eyes, Pierre was pursuing science for its own sake and not for personal glory.

Pierre was a confirmed bachelor, convinced that the opposite sex threatened to seduce him from the life of the laboratory, the only place where he could find fulfillment. He had not thought it possible to find a woman with whom he could discuss the work he loved in technical terms and who could understand what he was talking about.

Pierre fell in love with Marie—and remained in love with her until the day he died. As the weather turned warmer and Marie neared the end of her classes, she relaxed her all-work, no-play schedule. They walked together in the forests north of Paris, where the ground underfoot turned into a brilliant carpet of blue periwinkles. Pierre picked some of the lovely little flowers and showed Marie their petals to illustrate the symmetry in every form of nature. Another day as they were walking, he stopped unexpectedly to scoop up a small frog and startled Marie by depositing the soggy creature in her hand. "Now, really, Pierre!" Marie scolded.

After graduating second in her class, *magna cum laude* (with great distinction), and getting her second degree—

licence ès sciences mathématiques—Marie left for Warsaw in the summer of 1894. She had always expected that, once she had the education she needed, she would come back to live with her father and help her country regain its freedom. What she saw in Poland made Marie realize that any attempt to change the current situation would be overwhelming. The possibilities of accomplishing something in Paris in science were greater, and every discovery, no matter how small, represented a contribution to humanity.

While she was having second thoughts about her future, Pierre's letters, on cheap paper in his scrawled handwriting, pursued her. Most women of the day were happy to accept marriage and motherhood as their ultimate goal and stay in the niche where society put them. Not Marie. She sought self-fulfillment in her research and felt the need to prove her capabilities. This drive, however, did not mean she objected to love or raising a family. Marie was not playing hard-to-get with Pierre. She simply did not yet know her own mind. Pierre's competition was Poland, and he knew it.

Marie returned to Paris at the end of the summer to continue her commissioned work on the magnetic properties of steel. And Pierre continued to court her.

Finally Marie said yes. Bronya's mother-in-law gave Marie a wedding dress of her choice from a dressmaker in the neighborhood. As might be expected, Marie chose something practical. She did not select the conventional white gown. Instead she picked a navy wool suit that would not show dirt and which, together with its lighter blue, striped blouse, could be worn later in the laboratory. On July 26, 1895, Marie and Pierre had the simplest civil ceremony possible. There was no exchange of wedding rings, not even a wedding feast. The next morning, Pierre and Marie set off to explore the French countryside on their new bicycles, which had been purchased with money given to Marie for her trousseau by a cousin.

Shortly after their wedding, Pierre and Marie visited Pierre's parents at Sceaux. Here they are in the garden with their new bicycles.

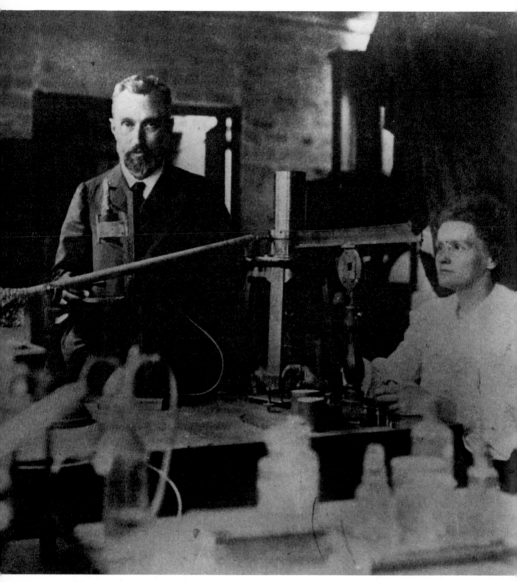

Pierre and Marie at work in their shed on the rue Lhomond. Pierre, who excelled at creating imaginative, makeshift apparatus, made many of Marie's instruments—including an ionization chamber made from a jelly can.

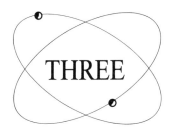

THREE

Madame Curie

1895-1901

Pierre could never be away from his laboratory for any great length of time, even during his honeymoon. By early September, Marie and Pierre were back in Paris. They found —on the fourth floor of an old building only a 15-minute walk from EPCI—a three-room apartment with a fine view of the tree-filled garden behind. Marie refused the furniture Pierre's family offered them because she intended to keep housework to a minimum. They had what they needed: only two chairs because they did not expect visitors, a white wooden table to work and eat at, plenty of bookshelves, and a bed. In the middle of the table was a small petrol lamp and a vase, which they always kept filled with fresh flowers. The walls were bare.

Marie was no more fond of cooking now than she had been before her marriage. But like everything else she did, if she was going to do it, she wanted to do it well. So she had Bronya teach her. However, absent-minded Pierre paid scant attention to what he put in his mouth. One night at dinner, when Marie asked him how he enjoyed his lamb chop, he looked at her in astonishment. "But I haven't tasted it yet." Then he noticed his empty plate.

Marie's initial purchase as a bride was a black account book in which she recorded all the money spent. They were living, for the time being, on Pierre's scant earnings so Marie could finish her commission to study the magnetic properties of different steels. Evenings found the petrol lamp burning late in the little apartment, with Marie and Pierre at opposite ends of the table, hard at work.

One of the few times the Curies were ever separated was two years after their wedding, in the summer of 1897, when Marie was pregnant. She was far from well, and Pierre could not leave Paris until classes were finished. So her father came from Poland and took her to a small fishing village in Brittany. The last thing one might expect the head-in-the-clouds, impractical Pierre to write about to his "dear little child whom I love so much" would be the needed baby clothes. But he did.

Marie's letters were equally affectionate: "My dear husband. Come quickly. I am awaiting you from dawn to dusk ...I love you with all my heart and press you in my arms. Your M." To please Marie, Pierre even made the effort—and it was a struggle—to write her in Polish. She replied in short simple phrases that he, as a beginner, might understand.

On September 12, 1897, Irène was born. Marie, like her sister Bronya, was determined to combine motherhood and marriage with a career. It never entered Marie's head that this was not feasible. She hired a wet nurse to nurse Irène and a maid to do the heaviest household chores. Then she began preparing for the next hurdle.

Although there was one *fräulein* in Germany who was well along with a thesis in chemistry, no European woman had yet completed a Ph.D. in science. But Marie was both determined and self-confident. In earning her Ph.D., she expected no allowances would be made for her gender. Indeed, Marie knew she had to overachieve and be superior to men in order for them to recognize her as an equal. She would also have to weather centuries of male prejudice.

The starting point for her Ph.D. was her doctoral thesis —a major paper that had to cover a subject that demanded original research. Both she and Pierre were excited about the mysterious rays discovered by the German professor Wilhelm Röntgen the year the Curies were married.

These unknown—hence the name "X"—rays were able to pass through opaque substances, such as wood and metal. With these mysterious X rays, Röntgen took a photograph of the bones of his wife's hand. When she held her hand in front of a screen, the rays passed through the flesh surrounding the bones. This photo caused a sensation worldwide.

The X-ray photo of Frau Röntgen's hand

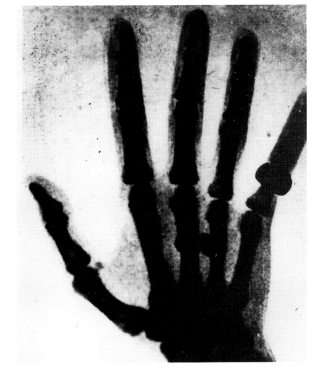

Professor Henri Becquerel, a colleague of the Curies, knew that for these rays, or radiation, to occur there had to be a source. He promptly started to search for it. Like his father and grandfather and great-grandfather, he specialized in fluorescence—that is, the ability of a substance to shine in the dark after exposure to light. He wrapped a photographic plate in black paper, and put a lump of uranium salts—a compound of other elements with uranium, which fluoresces after being exposed to light—on top. Because the next few days were cloudy, he set it aside in a desk drawer. Three days later, he developed the film anyway. To his astonishment, he discovered that the uranium salts had darkened the photographic plate. Whatever radiation the uranium salts were giving off did not depend on light and did not involve fluorescence. The uranium salts alone were giving off rays capable of penetrating matter.

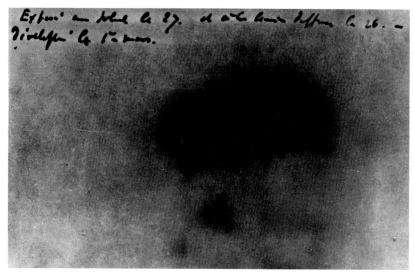

Becquerel's photographic plate, showing the discoloration made on it in the dark by uranium salts

Marie's decision to study the Becquerel rays was to be one of the most important of her entire life. It was to govern the rest of her career, link the Curie family intimately to the development of nuclear physics, and affect the entire world.

Once Marie had decided to study the Becquerel rays, she needed a place to work. The director of EPCI, where Pierre worked, came to the rescue with an unused, glass-paneled atelier on the rue Lhomond. Marie accepted gratefully. She could put up with the rain dripping down from the leaky roof and the unregulated changes in temperature, but she knew these conditions would pose a serious problem for the delicate instruments she would use. She later estimated that with proper equipment and an adequate laboratory, she and Pierre could have accomplished in two years what took them five.

Here, on December 16, 1897, Marie made her first notations in the same small, black-bound book that Pierre had been using for his own work. In the beginning, everything was recorded in Marie's neat hand. Intermingled here and there was an occasional margin note, a few figures, or a curve in Pierre's tiny scrawl to indicate how closely he was following her work. In roughly a year, an amazingly short amount of time, Marie and Pierre would find an answer to what they were seeking. Marie would be well on her way toward her doctorate and was starting the spadework for her Nobel-winning discovery.

Marie's first step was to determine whether anything other than uranium salts produced radiation similar to Becquerel's. The only known fact about his rays was that they betrayed their presence by making the air a conductor of electricity. So she decided to determine whether radiation was being produced by various samples of minerals. And, if so, how much. Since Marie had to manage with whatever equipment was at hand, she decided to use an early invention of the Curie brothers—their piezo-quartz electrometer —which was lying idle in the EPCI laboratory. The electrometer was made-to-order for measuring feeble electric currents with pinpoint accuracy. She painstakingly tested each mineral sample, one by one.

Within a few weeks, Marie determined that the rays' strength was in direct proportion to the amount of uranium in the sample. This was true whether the sample was solid or powdered, dry or wet. Nor was the amount of radiation affected by anything external like light or heat. She also determined that one other element—thorium—produced rays similar to those of uranium salts and other uranium compounds. Marie proceeded cautiously, repeating every stage of her work.

Up to this point, Marie's work had been painstaking but nothing exceptional. Now she made a leap of genius: the emission of rays must be a phenomenon occurring within the atom of uranium itself! Since thorium also gave off rays, this ability was not the property of a single element—a property only of pure uranium and its compounds—but an atomic property. Therefore, this property had to be given a name of its own. Marie coined the word "radioactivity" from the Latin *radius*, or "ray," for the property of atoms to emit rays. Any radioactive element would be called a "radioelement." Radioactivity was the first new property of matter to have been revealed since Newton discovered the law of gravity.

This disarmingly simple hypothesis was to be Marie's most important single contribution to science. With the understanding of radioactivity, the mysteries of the structure of the atom would be probed and opened up as the 20th century unfolded. A famous Nobel physicist would express it differently: "Pierre Curie's greatest discovery was Marie Sklodowska. Her greatest discovery was that radioactivity was atomic."

After examining hundreds of pure metals and their compounds—salts, oxides, and ores—Marie discovered that two uranium ores, pitchblende and chacolite, were also radioactive. To her amazement, the radiation from them was much stronger than she expected. A piece of crude pitchblende, which is a uranium oxide—a compound of uranium, oxygen, and other elements—had nearly four times the radioactivity of the pure uranium extracted from it. Chacolite had almost as much.

At first, she could not explain the results and thought she had made a mistake. The dust particles that were forever swirling around from her dirt floor might easily cause errors. Yet each time she redid her work she got the same results. During the long hours of solitary work, Marie puzzled over the problem.

As she and Pierre hurried to and fro on the narrow rue Lhomond, neighborhood shopkeepers could set their clocks, in the morning and at dusk, by the plainly dressed, somber pair, he tall and she small, always deep in grave discussion, trying to resolve Marie's puzzle. Although scientists believed that all the elements in uranium oxide were known, they must be mistaken. Something else must be present in so tiny a quantity that it had escaped detection until now. Marie herself had only been able to determine its presence because she was measuring the radioactivity of pitchblende, a uranium oxide. Since she could not identify the unknown substance that was causing the radiation, she reasoned that it must be a new element. Pierre was swept along by Marie's contagious enthusiasm. Attracted by the mystery surrounding her re-sults to date, he tabled his own research, which he was sandwiching in between his classes, to lend a hand.

On April 12, 1898, Marie's first report, announcing "the probable presence in pitchblende ore of a new element en-dowed with powerful radioactivity," was presented to the French Academy of Sciences. This was the starting point for the discovery of radium.

Pierre and Marie reasoned that even if the element re-sponsible for the rays existed in quantities so small that it had defied discovery to date, its radioactivity could guide them to it like a homing pigeon. Therefore, they must start by breaking down pitchblende and, after each step, keep only the radioactive fragment, discarding the rest, until they found what they were looking for.

On July 18, 1898, Marie threw a sweater across her shoulders and, clutching a vial with the latest fragment of pitchblende, hurried to the nearby laboratory of a colleague —a spectrographer. This man was able to identify each ele-ment by the specific rainbow-colored pattern, or spectrum, that an element shows when sparked by an electric current. No two elements ever have the same spectrum. That after-noon, when Marie rushed in, out of breath, and handed the spectrographer her latest specimen, there was enough substance in the glass vial—and it was pure enough—for the spectrographer to detect a spectral line he had never seen before. This proof was what Marie had been waiting to hear. The element in the vial was an unknown radioactive substance.

Because Marie was homesick, she and Pierre decided that, if the existence of this new substance was confirmed, they would name it "polonium," after Poland.

That same summer Marie received a welcome windfall — a prize given by the French Academy of Sciences. The money amounted to slightly more than Pierre's annual EPCI salary. So the minute classes were over, the family rented a peasant's cottage in the Auvergne in central France and shipped their bicycles south on the train. They took a few side trips to villages near the cottage, but were too tired to travel farther. After three unsuccessful attempts, Irène learned to be bathed in the river without crying. The little toddler went chasing

GrandPé (Dr. Curie) and Irène in July 1900

after the peasant's cat with wild war whoops. "She sings a great deal," Marie recorded in her journal.

Back home, Marie and Pierre soon discovered to their amazement that there must be not one but two unknown elements in pitchblende, both highly radioactive. On December 26, 1898, the French Academy of Science's *Comptes Rendus,* France's most important scientific review, carried Marie and Pierre's report on the probable existence of another new element. This they christened "radium"—also from the Latin *radius,* or ray. This report was published only a year after Marie had started work on her thesis, and six months after the discovery of polonium. Fast work by any standards.

To announce the probable existence of the two new elements, radium and polonium, was one thing. But nobody had yet set eyes on either of them. Marie now needed to determine the principal properties of radium and polonium, and to do so, each would have to be in its pure form. Her results to date indicated that radium was the more powerful of the two elements. Because the radiation given off from radium was stronger, it would be more readily detectable and easier to extract from pitchblende than polonium.

Marie and Pierre estimated that radium must consist of probably no more than 1/100 part of pitchblende. They were to learn that radium was less than 1/1,000,000 of a part. It would require about 50 tons of water and between 5 and 6 tons of chemicals to treat 1 ton of pitchblende and obtain 5 to 6 grains of radium—only 300 to 400 milligrams!

Since Pierre and Marie had to pay for it themselves, they needed to find a cheap, abundant source of pitchblende. What they were searching for was in the pitchblende residue that was discarded once uranium was extracted from uranium ore. Uranium ore was expensive, and the chief source in Europe was the St. Joachimsthal mines in Bohemia. Through a friend, the Curies were able to purchase some of the pitchblende residue for its transportation costs alone.

Because of the vast amounts of pitchblende they would be working with, more room was required. Nothing was available elsewhere. However, the tiny atelier they were using opened onto an unkempt back courtyard containing a ramshackle hangar, once used by the School of Medicine as a dissecting room. Its ceiling was shaky, its windows were ill-fitting and drafty, its taps dripped. The walls were of ruined plaster and partially glassed-in, as was the roof, and the dust from the floor posed a serious contamination problem. If the Curies wanted this shed, it was theirs. They moved in—gratefully.

The shed on the rue Lhomond

Marie and Pierre in 1904

When a great German chemist traveled from Berlin expressly to visit them and saw the hangar, he labeled it a cross between a stable and a potato cellar. Other well-known laboratories of the day were not much better. Yet Marie would remark, in her biography of Pierre, "it was in this miserable old shed that the best and happiest years of our life were spent, entirely consecrated to work."

Once the Curies had a place to put it, they sent for as much pitchblende as they could afford. Anxiously, Marie awaited its arrival. The day she heard a heavily laden, horse-drawn wagon grind to a halt on the rue Lhomond, she raced out, hatless and coatless, and directed the carter to the spot where the precious shipment could be unloaded. When the first grimy gunnysack was tossed to the ground, Marie was so excited to see its contents that her fingers kept fumbling with the cord tying it. Impatiently she yanked out a small pocket knife and slit one side. Black ore spilled every which way. Eagerly Marie reached down, grabbed a handful of ore mixed with pine needles from the forest floor where the mining company had dumped the residue, and hastened back inside. Her electrometer confirmed that the waste pitchblende was highly radioactive.

Here the slender woman in a dark dress covered with an acid-stained smock began the mammoth task of purifying the pitchblende. She would need to break down the chemical bonds between the elements present in pitchblende to extract pure radium. Like a persistent ant, she accumulated and stored ever more containers with compounds in various stages of purification. When Pierre was not busy with his classes, he helped. But his primary preoccupation was with the delicate tests necessary to determine radium's properties. False starts were made—and errors. Many days nothing seemed to work.

Marie could handle up to 20 kilograms of pitchblende at a time, enough to fill one of their largest cast-iron cauldrons. She was doing the work of a day laborer, keeping the fires going under the immense containers while she mixed the poisonous sludge round and round with a steel rod taller than herself.

There were no exhaust hoods to carry off the noxious fumes emitted by hydrogen sulfide and other substances that formed as she worked to isolate the elements in pitchblende. In order not to asphyxiate herself and Pierre, she had to tug and haul the boiling matter into the open courtyard to continue the distillation. When it snowed, she almost froze to death. When there was a real downpour, she had no choice but to cart everything back indoors and work there with all the windows open. And of course, when it rained, she also had to rush to move the open containers to avoid the splash of raindrops trickling down from the cracks overhead.

After weeks of back-breaking labor—refining and purifying—a cauldron of pitchblende was reduced to the contents of a small bowl of radium salts and set alongside others already filled. And Marie started the whole cycle over again with a fresh 20 kilograms of pitchblende. Small wonder her fingertips were red, cracking, and sore.

With all this intense activity, Marie and Pierre hardly went anywhere and rarely saw anyone except Dr. Curie and Irène. They used to see Bronya and her husband each Sunday. But the Dluskis had returned to Poland to establish their own sanatorium. No sooner had the sisters parted than Marie was writing for advice on everything from how to water the plants they had left behind to what to feed Irène. The toddler, proving to be a very fussy eater, wanted only milk tapioca.

Indeed, Irène was a little tyrant—a difficult, demanding child like many who have to share their parents with brothers and sisters. Irène's competition, however, was a laboratory. After Irène was tucked into bed and finally asleep, Marie and Pierre often walked back to EPCI. They would push open the creaking door of their makeshift laboratory and allow a few moments for their eyes to grow accustomed to the hangar's darkness. Looking round at the mysterious blue glow from each of the steadily increasing number of bottles and saucers lining the tables and simple plank shelves, Marie and Pierre were filled with a sense of awe. Taking Pierre's arm, Marie then would ease the door shut quietly, as if afraid

This photo, taken in the dark, shows the glow coming from a small container of radium.

she might break some magic spell, and they would head home. "These lights . . . suspended in the dark were always a new source of emotion and excitement for us."

After Pierre's mother died, Dr. Curie retired and moved in with Pierre and Marie. The Curies needed an extra bedroom, so Marie rented a small, two-story house in the south of Paris, not too far from the rue Lhomond. There was a tiny garden in back where Irène played and GrandPé—as Irène called her grandfather—cultivated flowers.

The years between 1900 and 1903 were the most creative of Marie's entire scientific life. The Curies published more scientific reports than at any other time. Some of the various scientific prizes Marie and Pierre continued to win supplemented their income. These awards also made the Paris scientific community aware of the Curies' increasing prominence on the international scene. Pierre accepted an assistant professorship at the Sorbonne.

About the same time, Marie found a teaching job. Twice a week, she set off on the steam tramway that crossed the Seine and proceeded at a snail's pace to the suburb of Sèvres. She got off at the beginning of a long driveway leading to the grilled entryway of a lovely, walled estate. Within was a former porcelain factory that now served as the École Normale Supérieure de Sèvres for girls. A government boarding school, Sèvres had been recently established to recruit and prepare women to teach in the state-run girls' schools. *Sèvriennes*—as the students were called—were not considered capable of instructing young men. The entrance examinations were extremely difficult. In return for their education, which was free, the sèvriennes were obligated, upon graduation, to 10 years of teaching.

This teaching position at Sèvres offered Marie her first salary since coming to Paris. She liked working with her bright students in their early 20s, and she enjoyed her contacts with the outstanding staff. During her stay at Sèvres, some of the most eminent French scholars also taught there. Marie's appointment created a sensation. A woman! Imagine! And she did not even have her Ph.D. yet! But she had discovered radium. And she had recently passed, in first place, the *Concours d'Agrégation*, which gave her a certificate to teach secondary education to girls.

Normally, the moment a teacher entered the front door, a bell rang to warn the sèvriennes of her arrival. But Marie quickly established a warm relationship with the four girls in her first class, and they watched eagerly for her from the window. As soon as they caught a glimpse of the slight, somberly clad figure hurrying down the driveway lined with chestnut trees, they ran to take their places in the lecture hall. On warm days, the girls waited for her outside in the courtyard. How the time flew in Marie's classes! The lunch bell rang and no one stirred. Teacher and pupils were too absorbed to hear. Then, suddenly, Marie realized the time. Her pupils rushed off to eat, while she swallowed a cup of tea and walked back down to await the tram.

Marie was shocked by her pupils' poor scientific preparation. She deplored the school's inadequate laboratory and the total lack of practical work offered the girls. She resolved to remedy this situation at once. Marie took great pains to prepare her lectures. Although she was hired to teach physics for only one-and-a-half hours, twice a week, she quickly doubled this time without extra charge. She added two other courses, differential and integral calculus, which she considered essential for intelligent, well-educated young women.

Marie frequently brought to class pieces of equipment that Pierre had modified, or even constructed from scratch, especially for her pupils. They considered "Madame" their role model. They had quickly realized that her reserved manner was only a mask to hide her timidity and warm heart. Marie's normally serious expression was often transformed into a smile at some of their naive remarks. She was well aware of their capabilities. One day, to instill in them a love for research as well as for teaching, Marie apologetically took time from Pierre's overloaded schedule by bringing the class to visit him in his laboratory. They were thrilled at the prospect of meeting this famous man, the husband of their admired, beloved teacher.

The sèvriennes watched spellbound as Pierre showed them how some of the instruments functioned, explaining everything in his grave, slow voice. Then he switched off the lights so his attentive audience might watch a glass tube glow as it was filled with radon, the gas that emanated from radium.

Inside the shed on the rue Lhomond where Marie did her research that led to the discovery of radium

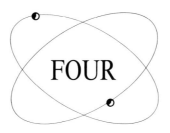

FOUR

The First Nobel

1901-1904

Marie blamed her off-again, on-again health and Pierre blamed his acute leg pains on their backbreaking schedules. Certainly, overwork played a contributing role. But the notion that radiation might pose a serious health risk never crossed their minds. Nor would it occur to anyone for a considerable amount of time to come. So the Curies had no reason to take special precautions. Should radioactive concentrates get spilled on the floor, the mess was mopped up with any rag at hand. The rag was then tossed in the refuse pail until the next day or whenever the garbage was carted out.

Unknown to Marie and Pierre, their poorly ventilated hangar at EPCI posed a lethal danger. Their unprotected bodies were daily absorbing deadly radiation from radon, the gas that radium emitted. Radon was capable of seeping through cork and rubber, so it was escaping from the improperly stoppered glass flasks in which radium was stored. These radium-related factors have since become recognized agents for a variety of human ailments, including different cancers and damaged bone marrow.

Radium had one immediate physical effect of which both Curies were already painfully aware. Their hardened, damaged fingertips resulted from constant handling of radium salts, and they would never completely heal. Marie spent the rest of her life unconsciously rubbing her fingertips together, over and over again.

German scientists who were beginning to test radium's rays discovered they had other effects on the human body. A colleague of Marie's got a burn on his stomach when he absentmindedly tucked a vial of radium salts, which she had loaned him, into his vest pocket and promptly forgot about it. Further research proved that radium destroyed the sick cells in skin cancer, and when the skin regenerated, it was healthy. However, only certain types of cancers were affected.

This research marked the beginning of radiotherapy. "Curietherapy," as it was soon called in France, was to develop into an important branch of medicine. It was the first step toward modern radiation treatment of cancer. More and more doctors started borrowing infinitesimal amounts of radium and radon gas from the Curies for use on their patients. Tremendously radioactive, radium became the miracle drug of the day.

Marie refused to permit her enjoyable two half-days a week at Sèvres to divert her one second longer than necessary from her research. As she approached the final stages of radium purification, there was still no other researcher attempting the same task, because what Marie was doing was strenuous and tedious. Ambitious Marie wanted to be the first to produce pure radium, not just the radium chloride and bromide she already had. She was convinced that other scientists would not believe she had found a new element unless it was in its pure form.

Meanwhile, the existence of the new element could be proven and studied if she had enough of its compound, radium chloride. So on March 28, 1902, a blustery spring day, Marie hastened back to the spectrographer. Excitedly she thrust a tube containing about one-tenth of a gram of radium chloride, which resembled ordinary table salt, into his hand. Was it pure enough? Yes! Triumphantly, four months later, Marie announced the weight of radium. Its chemical biography was complete.

The traditional approach to pure science dictated that a scientist's duty was to learn, explore, and publish without thought of profit but simply to benefit humanity. Marie and Pierre felt it unworthy to do otherwise, especially when a basic discovery of science was in question. "Disinterested" was the highest praise that either one of these traditional scientists could ever bestow. They were generous in loaning samples of their precious radioactive salts to qualified people. Although worldwide patents would have been worth a fortune, nothing was done to protect the detailed process they developed for purifying pitchblende and isolating radium.

Despite Marie's great success in the laboratory, there were many troubled nights in the Curie household. Marie was sleepwalking, perhaps in part because of her grief over the death of her father in Poland. And sometimes Pierre lay awake moaning with terrible leg pains that medicine did not relieve. Worried and frightened, Marie watched helplessly when these attacks occurred. When the pair got up in the morning, Pierre was weak and Marie was exhausted. From the sidelines, old Dr. Curie was a concerned spectator.

And what about five-year-old Irène? The house was small, and even though children usually sleep soundly, she must have heard what was going on or been awakened by her father's crying out. What did she make of it? Was she frightened at her mother's sleepwalking? At her father being racked by pain?

That autumn, Marie brought her Sèvres class of four home for tea. None of their other teachers had ever done such a thing, and the girls were thrilled. Giggling nervously as they walked up the boulevard Kellerman, they wondered what Madame would be like at home. They were also looking forward to meeting her daughter. They had talked a lot about Irène among themselves. How did it feel to be the daughter of a famous couple? Whom would she resemble?

Marie smiled when she saw them, dressed in their Sunday best from the tips of the flower-trimmed, straw boaters perched on top of their heads to the toes of their high-buttoned shoes. It was not so many years since Marie had been a student herself. She could imagine the excitement as well as the uneasiness that the girls must have felt.

Marie Curie is surrounded by her sèvriennes on the steps at the École Normale Supérieure de Sèvres. Eugénie Feytis is at the left.

Where was Irène? the girls asked politely, after a few moments of conversation. Irène was peeking at them from the other side of the living room door. Stubbornly she refused to join them. When the child at last ventured out, she made a beeline for her mother and hid in her skirts. From that secure position, with her chubby arms tightly encircling Marie's legs, the rosy-cheeked little girl glared at the intruders. She was not shy but on the defensive. She regarded the appearance of these big girls with stormy uneasiness. What were they doing invading Irène's home, usurping Mé's time? Marie was "Mé" and Pierre "Pé" to Irène. She refused to let the big girls steal her mother's attention from her. From time to time that afternoon she repeated to her mother in a firm, grave voice that reminded the girls of her father: "You must take notice of me."

Marie made a great effort to make the girls feel more comfortable. She asked each of them personal questions to draw them out so she might get to know them better. At last it was time for tea. Even little Irène was interested in that. Her hostility disappeared as she skipped ahead into the modest dining room.

Marie was preparing, at last, to finish her Ph.D. She and Pierre were also starting to pay the price for becoming better known. Certain official engagements were now impossible to refuse. These events were one more drain on their strength, and Marie was losing weight. When a close colleague met Marie at a Physics Society meeting he was shocked at her appearance. He wrote a 10-page letter pleading with them to change their habits before it was too late. She and Pierre did not give enough time to their meals. "It is not necessary to mix scientific preoccupations into every instant of your life.... Don't you love Irène? It seems to me that I wouldn't

*GrandPé and Irène
in 1903*

prefer the idea of reading a [scientific] paper...to getting what my body needs and of looking at such an agreeable little girl. Give her a kiss for me. If she were a bit older, she would think as I do and she would tell you all this. Think of her a little."

For all the loving care doting old Dr. Curie lavished on his granddaughter, GrandPé was not the same as Mé and Pé. No one but Mé could undress Irène at night—when Marie was home. Then Irène insisted that Mé must stay with her, talking or reading, no matter how tired Marie might be, until the six-year-old fell asleep. Should Irène awaken, she would call "Mé! Mé!" in a demanding voice. Marie would return and sit alongside Irène again in the darkness until sleep once more claimed her.

Marie's required thesis for her Ph.D., "Research on Radio-active Substances," was finally finished and approved by her examining committee. Containing a summary of her entire work to date on radioactivity, this report ranks as Marie's most outstanding publication and belongs among the classics of science. For it depicts the beginnings of the new field that led ultimately to nuclear physics.

On June 25, 1903, Marie appeared in the sun-drenched students' hall at the Sorbonne for the oral examination that was the final requirement for her doctorate. Old Dr. Curie was there with Pierre. Bronya had come west for the occasion. Marie also had seats reserved for her sèvriennes. She had gotten them excused from class to attend. Marie had been coaxed by Bronya into buying a new dress. She chose a dark gray, not because that color happened to be stylish that season but because, like black, the color of her one other dress, it did not show dirt. She could also wear it in the laboratory.

Marie was uneasy, as usual, about speaking before a number of people. However, she was calmness personified where the examination itself was concerned. Marie was never modest about her own work. She knew her subject better than her three examiners. At the end, she was accorded the title of "doctor of physical science," *summa cum laude* (with highest distinction).

Marie was the first woman to get her doctorate in France. It was the only way to success in her chosen field. She had achieved her goal, and in so doing, she had detected the presence of two new elements and isolated them. She was a brilliant woman, whose stubbornness had helped her overcome enormous handicaps.

Irène was old enough to start school that fall, but no school in the neighborhood satisfied her parents. So the six-year-old entered a school some distance away but not so far that Marie could not occasionally walk Irène there en route to the rue Lhomond. Sometimes Marie managed to catch a glimpse of her daughter in the afternoon in the Parc Montsouris where GrandPé or the nurse took her daily to play.

Then, in mid-November 1903, Marie and Pierre learned that they and Henri Becquerel had been jointly awarded the Nobel Prize for physics for their work on radioactivity. This prize, established in 1900, brought Marie and Pierre international glory and changed their lives dramatically. Photographers and journalists hounded them everywhere. Marie termed their notoriety "a disaster."

The Curies' half of the prize money, together with the money Marie was shortly awarded for another prize, removed the family from any further financial problems. They spent only a small amount: a loan to her sister Bronya and her husband; another to Pierre's brother, Jacques; a few gifts. Marie, being Marie, did not even buy a new hat, but she did repaper one room and install a modern bathroom in their home. The rest of the money was placed in French investments and in bonds of the city of Warsaw.

There were many days now when Marie and Pierre were almost too busy to breathe. Young Irène had difficulty adjusting to the new state of affairs. She did not welcome the fact that her parents went out at night more frequently. She had a hard time recognizing Mé, in her one evening dress, when she left for some official affair. The whiteness of her bare shoulders and arms made her mother's fine ash-blond hair look even fairer, her deep gray eyes bigger, and she seemed more beautiful than ever in her daughter's adoring eyes.

One of Marie's sèvriennes, Eugénie Feytis, became a family favorite, especially with Irène. She came to the house frequently. Sometimes she took Irène to Sèvres, where the girl wanted to see Eugénie's room. Irène also wanted to visit Mé's lecture hall and laboratory and insisted on walking in the park to locate the sites of the different photos the sèvriennes were always taking of their beloved teacher. Irène now realized that she must share her Mé with these other big girls, and it helped to be able to see where her mother spent her time when she was at Sèvres. Irène was equally interested in the school's natural history museum and was fascinated by the size of a mammoth's tooth on display there. She once asked Eugénie gravely—she always spoke gravely, this small girl, as if she had never had a childhood—"Have you ever seen a mammoth?"

"No. The beast lived a long time ago."

Anxious for an eyewitness account of the creature, Irène thought a moment. "Very well. I shall ask GrandPé."

A serious, reserved child, Irène was not used to shows of affection. Since Marie had not been brought up with any —partially because of her mother's fear of transmitting tuberculosis—she felt no need for it with her own child. So it was no wonder that the girl did not enjoy being hugged and kissed by her mother's pupils, who always made a big fuss over her. Even as she grew older, Irène was never really sociable, except with an intimate few.

On October 1, 1904, in time for the upcoming school year, Pierre was promoted to professor of physics at the Sorbonne. A modest laboratory was to be constructed for him, although it would still lack many essentials. More importantly, Pierre was given funds for three paid workers: an assistant, a lab boy, and a laboratory chief—the last clearly specified as Marie. Finally Marie Curie had an official title authorizing her to work in Pierre's laboratory, and she was to receive her first pay for research.

Irène and Pierre in the country at Saint-Rémy-lès-Chevreuse in September 1904

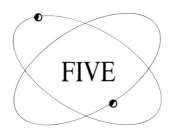

FIVE

Catastrophe

1904-1906

On December 6, 1904, Ève Denise was born. Marie was delighted to have another daughter. She had wanted a second child badly. Irène promptly hurried in to inspect her sister. Naturally the new arrival absorbed the lion's share of Mé's time, a development that did not suit Irène.

In the spring of 1906, the Seine was so high that Parisians walked along the *quais* to gape at the muddy, swirling waters. But by April, the weather turned lovely.

For the long Easter weekend, Pierre and Marie took the two children out to nearby Saint-Rémy-lès-Chevreuse. Marie had rented a little cottage here because she believed it was important for the girls get away from smoky Paris. On Easter morning, they could hear the church bells of the old abbey of Port Royal ringing as they set out for their daily walk. Ève perched contentedly on her father's shoulders. It was hot, so Irène stripped off her jumper and started chasing butterflies. She was a comical figure in a mismatched girl's undershirt and boy's underpants with a long, green-handled net bigger than she. The next day, Monday, the quartet picked periwinkles and buttercups in the swamp. Then, after a quick dinner, Pierre caught a train back to Paris.

On Wednesday evening, Marie returned with the two girls. On Thursday, April 19, it was raining, dark, and gloomy.

Pierre had a busy schedule and rushed off early, while Marie was upstairs dressing the girls. After a luncheon meeting, Pierre unfurled his big black umbrella and headed down the rue Dauphine toward the Seine and a session at the French Academy. The street, like others in that old section of Paris, was not wide, and it was cluttered at that hour. There was the usual amount of traffic at the intersection of the *quais* with the bridge. A heavy, horse-drawn dray with a load of military uniforms clattered across the river, and its pair of horses broke into a trot coming down the narrow rue Dauphine, head-on toward Pierre.

Suddenly, without looking to the right or left, absent-minded Pierre decided to cross over. It was all over in seconds. Death was instant. The police commissioner promptly notified the minister of the interior.

When Marie returned home late, old Dr. Curie told her the terrible news. There was a long silence. "Pierre is dead?" How could it be! "Are you sure?" She went next door to the Perrins' to tell Irène, who was playing there, that Pé had been in a bad accident. He would need a lot of quiet. So Marie arranged to have Irène stay at the Perrins' for the next few days.

During the next hours, callers never stopped coming, beginning with the president of France. Pierre's brother, Jacques, arrived the next morning from Montpellier. Marie purposely advanced the day of the funeral to avoid any official government participation. Pierre's services must be private, the way he had preferred to live his life.

Pierre was buried in the countryside where he had spent a large part of his youth, in the small cemetery dominating the slopes of Sceaux. There was no priest, no sermon. At the end of the simplest of services, Marie abruptly seized a sheaf of flowers resting near the tomb. Oblivious to anything and anybody, she broke off the flowers slowly and methodically, one by one, and spread them over the grave.

Late Sunday afternoon, Irène was playing with Aline Perrin when Marie arrived. In black from head to toe, pale and icy-looking, she had come to tell her daughter the terrible truth. Irène acted as if she did not hear what her mother was saying and continued the game the two girls had started. Irène was not too young to understand. But the realization that she would never see Pé again had not yet penetrated. Marie was barely out the front door when Irène burst into tears and asked to be taken home.

As family and friends worried about what was to become of Marie, a widow with two small children to support, the government suggested a national pension. Marie, however, was too proud and too independent to accept favors from anyone. She was perfectly capable of supporting herself and her family.

Tears did not come easily for Marie. Even her closest friends were shut out; she could only confide her feelings to Pierre. "Everything is over...; it is the end of everything, everything, everything..." she wrote in a diary she began a few days later and addressed to Pierre.

Before the end of May, tradition and custom were swept aside when the minister of public instruction offered Pierre's chair to Marie with the title of assistant professor and a salary. Here was a new challenge for Marie—the first post in higher education in France to be given to a woman. Within a month of Pierre's death, the columns of neat figures in her laboratory workbooks began to lengthen. Marie was back at work, purifying radium metal.

Marie with Ève (left) *and Irène* (right) *in the garden at Sceaux in 1908*

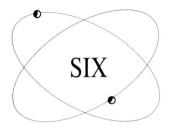

SIX

The Illustrious Widow

1906-1914

Marie lost not only a husband. She also lost her closest colleague. Gradually the laboratory resumed its dominant role in her life. Marie was determined not to neglect the delicate isolation of radium. Her success in doing so was to constitute her most important scientific work after Pierre's death. Dawn was often breaking before she hung up her coarse, stained smock on its wooden peg in the laboratory and bicycled homeward.

Marie took increasing pleasure in the company of her growing girls and did her best, in her own way, to give them a normal home life. The tree she decorated for them each Christmas—with garlands, colored candles, and gilded nuts—was just like the one Marie knew as a girl in Poland. It was long remembered by starry-eyed Irène and Ève.

Nine-year-old Irène was shy like her father. His death was a profound shock for which she vainly sought an explanation. But Marie was too wrapped in her own grief to recognize this. The girl kept watching for her adored mother to smile again. Irène did not realize that for Marie she was simultaneously a precious blessing and a cruel reminder of a life that was gone forever.

Fortunately, old Dr. Curie was there to help Irène overcome her misery. GrandPé, with his twinkling blue eyes

Nine-year-old Irène holding two-year-old Ève

peering down at her from underneath the tattered brim of an old straw hat, understood the sad child's need for special attention and affection. His cheerfulness was good for the whole family. With GrandPé in charge, Marie left the house each day with less worry.

In the summer of 1906, Marie's sister Hela Szalay came from Warsaw with her daughter Hania, who was almost Irène's age, and took Irène to the seashore. Irène kept her mother posted on her daily activities there. GrandPé, acting as Ève's secretary, wrote Irène:

"Eu, eu, eu, eu—Ève."

"My dear Irène, my dear big grand-daughter. I am sending you Ève's letter... I think you will recognize her style."

With so many new responsibilities, Marie was forced to give up teaching at Sèvres, much as she hated to. Early on Monday morning, November 5, 1906—the first day she assumed Pierre's classes—Marie went out to Sceaux to visit his grave.

Meantime, several hundred people were already gathered on the Place de la Sorbonne long before the school's gates opened at 1:00 P.M. In five minutes, the small physics amphitheater, which could seat 200, was full. Others were vainly trying to push their way in. History was being made today by Marie Curie. Her lecture would be the first ever given there by a woman, let alone to a class of advanced students. It marked "a Great Victory for Feminism," as the *Paris Journal* trumpeted across its front page. Present were reporters, photographers, prominent scientists, celebrities, and, of course, Pierre's students—now Marie's students. Her former sèvriennes were seated in reserved seats in the front row. She had gotten authorization for the girls to attend her fall lectures to make up for their spring classes, which had been canceled following Pierre's tragic accident.

At 1:30 sharp, Marie entered, almost furtively. She bowed her head slightly in acknowledgment of the huge ovation. The stark severity of the simple, unadorned, black mourning dress made her slender body look thinner and more fragile, her pale coloring more like alabaster. Marie laid out her papers and placed her watch alongside. Her lips pressed tightly together, she stood holding onto the long, apparatus-laden table with one hand, as if to steady herself. She kept shuffling papers with the other hand until there was silence. Then Marie began at the exact spot where Pierre had left off.

Marie reasoned that a change of scenery might do her family good. So they moved to the lovely ancient town of

Sceaux, where Pierre had lived with his family before their marriage and where he was buried. Sceaux was still in open country—an ideal environment for two growing girls. But the move meant a considerable sacrifice on Marie's part. Instead of being able to walk or bicycle to work, she would have to hurry to catch a slow commuter train for the half-hour ride into Paris.

Her children and her work saved Marie's sanity during those first years of widowhood. Irène and Ève clung to Mé wildly the little she was at Sceaux. If Marie did not give them much time, it was because she did not have many hours to give. There were few outward signs of warmth. But she never neglected an illness or a birthday, although birthdays were more often celebrated apart than together as Irène was growing up.

Old Dr. Curie became Irène's closest comrade. She loved to go on daily walks with him or curl up by the hour in a chair in his bedroom. She was already crazy about mathematics. When Irène was at the seashore, Marie ended her letters to Irène with algebraic equations to be solved, rather than kisses. Irène was at an age at which her education must be taken seriously. Marie had strong ideas on the subject and did not approve of the current educational system.

A number of her Sorbonne colleagues with young children—among them the Perrins and the Langevins—felt the same way. So they set up their own school. The "Cooperative," as it came to be called, started that fall. Jean Perrin taught chemistry to the 10 privileged children at the Sorbonne, Paul Langevin taught them mathematics, and Henriette Perrin taught them French history and literature. Marie was now giving the world's first course on radioactivity, but every Thursday it was her turn to work with the

Irène gently touches Mé's badly scarred fingertips, damaged by handling radium.

children in an empty room in the physics building. Here Irène got her first glimpse of Mé's exciting other world.

One day the class dipped bicycle ball-bearings in ink. Then they placed them on a slanted tabletop, where they verified the law of falling bodies by describing a parabola. Another time Marie gave the children a lesson in common sense. Taking a jug of boiling water off a burner, she asked the inquisitive youngsters what was the best way to keep the water hot. They bombarded her with a wide range of ingenious ideas. "Well," replied Marie, smiling. "This is what I'd do." And she put the lid on.

Attending the Cooperative in which her own mother taught meant that Irène saw more of her. Her relationship with Mé assumed deeper meaning. The following year, when her daughters returned to the Normandy seashore, Marie managed a short vacation with them.

As Irène approached 13, it was time for her to begin a more formal education. Sometime during that summer, Marie found time to give Irène and a friend algebra lessons to get the girls better prepared. One day Mé asked Irène a simple question. Her daughter had not been listening and could only reply, "I don't know."

"What do you mean, you don't know? How can you be so stupid?" Indignantly, Marie reached over and tossed Irène's notebook out the open window. If Marie could take the time from her busy schedule to teach the pair, Irène owed it to her mother to listen.

"I'm sorry," Irène mumbled, guiltily. Ashamed, she rushed downstairs to retrieve the notebook. Never again did Marie have to reprimand Irène for lack of attention.

Marie proposed the establishment of a radium institute to develop the new science of radioactivity. It seemed logical to combine such a laboratory under Marie with the existing Pasteur laboratory because of radium's medical applications. The Pasteur, named after the French scientist who discovered the treatment for rabies and developed a process for sterilizing milk, was a laboratory for biological research, including radiotherapy—or "Curietherapy." The Curie and Pasteur pavilions—two physically independent units— were to be known together as the Institut du Radium de l'Université de Paris. Marie was determined that this institute should become a world-renowned center in its field—a memorial truly worthy of Pierre.

In February 1910, snow covered Paris. At the Jardin des Plantes, the giraffe—Irène's special favorite among the animals at the zoo—died of the extreme cold. That same month GrandPé also passed away. His death was very hard on 13-year-old Irène. Twice already, in her young life, Irène had lost someone dear to her.

There was no need for Marie to change into mourning black. She had never taken it off.

When Irène again spent the month of August at the seashore with Aunt Hela and Hania, Marie put in a brief appearance. After she left, Irène wrote: "WHEN ARE YOU COMING BACK? . . . I shall be so happy when you come because I badly need someone to caress . . . I have made a fine paper envelope to hold your letters. There is only one in it."

In the fall of 1910, Irène entered the Collège de Sévigné, a private school in the heart of Paris with a superior mathematics program. Both she and Ève would have to earn their own living when they were older. Marie stressed that they should be proud of their independence and their ability to support themselves. Irène went to the head of her science class immediately. She shocked the other girls the day she explained to them, biologically, how babies were made and came into the world.

During the entire four years since Pierre's death, Marie had been plodding away at isolating radium metal. Finally, in an extremely dangerous, delicate operation, she got a tiny speck of pure radium metal. Soon afterward she also succeeded in isolating pure polonium.

Marie was beginning to amass honorary degrees and scientific society memberships from different countries. She made an increasing number of trips abroad, anxious to gain prestige for the future Curie Institute. Marie took her two daughters to Italy in the spring of 1911 when she attended a scientific conference there. And when Irène had summer vacation, Marie sent the pair to visit Bronya and Casimir Dluski at their sanatorium at Zakopane. This visit gave the girls a chance to become acquainted with the rest of their mother's Polish family.

Even there, study was not completely forgotten. Irène had a half-hour German lesson each morning and worked religiously on her algebra and trigonometry. When Irène suddenly fell ill, she was once more a lonely girl who wanted her mother. "Oh, how I would have liked to have you here while I was sick! . . . Your b-b-b-big Irène."

In the fall of 1911, the Belgian philanthropist Ernest Solvay invited the world's leading physicists to Brussels. Marie was among the 30-odd present at this, the first of numerous Solvay physics conferences. So was Albert Einstein. In 1905 he had forged another vital link in the chain of scientific evolution and heralded in the atomic age with his groundbreaking theory of relativity. His equation—$E = mc^2$,

Albert Einstein (left) *and Marie Curie* (right) *at the International Committee of Intellectual Cooperation in 1925*

Ernest Rutherford, a Nobel laureate and a devoted life-long friend of Marie's

where E is energy, m mass, and c the speed of light—spelled out the relationship between mass and energy. It helped explain radiation by providing the key to the tremendous energy locked in the atom.

The famed New Zealand physicist Ernest Rutherford was also present. He had already discovered that there were two types of uranium rays—alpha and beta. In addition, with the loan of a radioactive compound from Marie and Pierre, Rutherford and an associate were able to explain the phenomenon of radioactivity. Their "disintegration" theory was the most important contribution to the history of radioactivity since Marie's discovery of radium and her revolutionary hypothesis that radioactivity was an atomic property.

Four years Marie's junior, Rutherford had the unenviable task of trying to overcome her stubborn insistence that the International Radium Standard she was asked to prepare should remain in her own laboratory. One evening the burly man spent until midnight in her suite, spewing tobacco ash and burnt matches all over the rug, as he strode to and fro, drawing on his pipe—and arguing. Striving to control his "By thunders, Madame!" Rutherford lowered his booming voice to what would be a normal level for others. Then he bent down to speak earnestly to the small figure in black, sitting ramrod straight on the couch.

He reported, "It is going to be a ticklish business to get the matter arranged satisfactorily.... Mme Curie is rather a difficult person to deal with. She has the advantages and at the same time the disadvantages of being a woman." A compromise was ultimately worked out. As agreed upon, the name "curie" was adopted for the new unit of measurement.

In November 1911, Marie received a telegram from Stockholm informing her that she had won a second Nobel Prize. Marie was the first scientist to be crowned twice. The first time, Marie shared the Nobel—in physics—with her husband and Henri Becquerel for the discovery of radioactivity. This time she won it alone—in chemistry—for the preparation of her one gram of pure radium.

Even the momentous news of this second Nobel award did not completely silence a story, which may have been true, in the Paris scandal sheets linking the widowed Marie with Paul Langevin—a famous, longtime colleague who was separated from his wife. Disturbed by this investigation into her private life, Marie was again losing weight. Her friends worried about her health as much as about her state of mind. They wondered if she would be able to make the strenuous 48-hour trip to Stockholm in December to collect her Nobel award.

Irène and Bronya, the doctor in the family, accompanied Marie. When Marie stood to receive the Nobel medal and leather-bound certificate from King Gustav V in the great

hall of prizes in the royal palace, she was her usual, conspic-
uous self. Dressed in simple unadorned black lace, she stood
out amid that glittering galaxy of men awash in multi-
ribboned medals and women dripping elaborate jewelry. The
city reminded her of her happy past with Pierre, and the
memories exacted a toll. Only fierce determination kept Marie
on her feet. By the time she reached Paris, she collapsed
and fell into a deep depression.

Home now was on the fourth floor at #36 Quai de
Béthune, on the Île St. Louis in the Seine, within comfortable walking distance of the Sorbonne. Irène missed her own
private garden in their large yard at Sceaux. But the move
saved Marie the time-consuming, daily commuting. A bridge,

#36 Quai de Béthune. Marie's apartment is on the fourth floor.

the Pont de la Tournelle, connected the bohemian and academic world of the Left Bank with this quiet, sedate haven. The Quai de Béthune was anchored to the past by its severe, gray stone houses, untouched since the 17th century.

From an architectural point of view, the new apartment was superb. Of course, there was no elevator. The great expanse of shining inlaid floors was covered with a few scatter rugs from Polish peasants' looms and served as a vast skating rink for Irène's black cat. The huge, high-ceilinged rooms overpowered Marie's humble furniture, which looked lost amid so much splendor. Yet she never added a stick more. The tall windows that had formerly been draped in rich damasks remained bare except for thin net. The overall effect was one of icy discomfort, and the only room that ever appeared lived-in was Marie's workroom with its clutter of books and papers and her picture of Pierre. Ève's bedroom never looked the same two weeks in a row, because she was forever redecorating it. Irène never gave two thoughts to where she slept, provided there was a bed.

How much of Marie's intermittent high fever and assorted ailments could be traced to overexposure to radiation is unknown. At the end of March, she was operated on for kidney problems. A long convalescence followed. Toward the end of June, Marie suffered a relapse and was taken to a sanatorium in the Savoy Alps for a month. Irène's letters to Marie show her increasing maturity—and sense of humor. Commenting on the political situation in England, the girl observed: "I have...seen that an English Minister is almost killed every day...by the English suffragettes, but it seems to me that the[y]...have not found a brilliant way of proving they are capable of voting." Her health restored, Marie resumed teaching classes in January 1913.

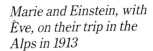

Marie and Einstein, with
Ève, on their trip in the
Alps in 1913

Marie had met Albert Einstein at the first Solvay physics conference and was impressed by both him and his work. They decided to go on a holiday with their families. The walking trip through the Alps was a great success, and the two Curie girls got along famously with Hans, the older Einstein boy, who was Ève's age. Marie enjoyed herself thoroughly, as did Einstein, who would refer to her as "the one person whom fame has not corrupted."

There was a lot of shop talk in German. Einstein was struck by Irène's intelligence and became her lifelong friend. The girls were amused at the way he wandered absentmindedly among the boulders, so deep in conversation with Mé that he walked alongside deep crevasses and toiled up the steep rocks without noticing them. One day, the young people howled with laughter when he suddenly stopped dead, seized Marie's arm and demanded: "What I need to know is exactly what happens to the passengers in an elevator when it falls into emptiness." The imaginary fall in an elevator posed problems of relativity. There would be no gravitational pull, so the passengers would float.

The amount of travel Marie was undertaking now was a far cry from the cloistered life she once led with Pierre. One minute she was in Manchester, England, for an honorary degree. Next she went to Warsaw for the ground breaking of the Polish radium institute, whose honorary director she was. But once work actually started on the Curie Institute, it was not as easy for Marie to get away. She insisted that the original budget include a salary for a gardener. And before the foundations were completely laid, she planted willows in the small garden that was to be in the courtyard uniting the Curie and Pasteur pavilions. For Marie believed that laboratories should have big windows and the people working in

The Curie Pavilion, facing the rue Pierre-et-Marie-Curie

them should be able to look out at something green and growing. Nothing escaped Marie's attention. She conducted a daily inspection tour, even climbing scaffoldings when necessary. Each Friday afternoon, she participated in the on-site meeting of the architect, the contractors, and the construction workers.

Forming a nucleus of research workers, molding them into a productive team, and keeping them financed and equipped was to absorb the major portion of Marie's life. The phenomenal success of radium in the treatment of certain cancers caused demand for radium to far outstrip the supply. Even though the University of Vienna was now producing considerable quantities of radium, the price of radioactive materials was sky-high. The Curie Institute itself cost 800,000 gold francs to build—only 50,000 gold francs more than a gram of radium.

Early in the summer of 1914, Marie again sent her girls with the Polish cook and governess to L'Arcouest, the peaceful Brittany fishing village that was the summer retreat of a number of Marie's Sorbonne colleagues. She planned to join them later, after her duties at the end of the school year were completed and she made the final move into the Curie. Marie was used to staying alone in the summer, rattling around by herself in the big empty apartment. After working late, she came home, went over the mail, and read Irène's letters. Each letter between the pair, whether from Irène or to her, ended on a mathematical note. "The derivatives are coming along all right," the young woman wrote. "The inverse functions are adorable. On the other hand, I can feel my hair stand on end when I think of the theorem of Rolle, and Thomas's formula"—a formula that Irène had previously described as "the ugliest thing I know."

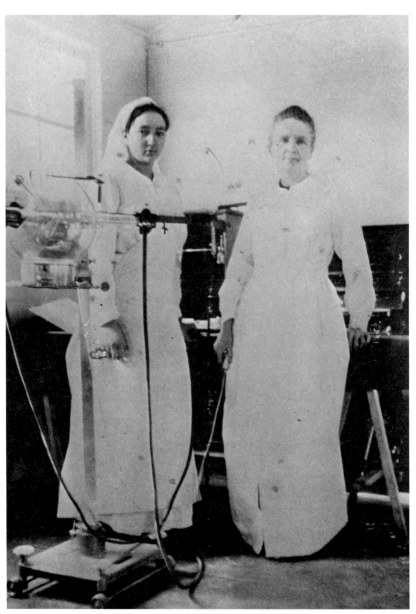

Irène and Marie with radiological apparatus in the Belgian hospital of Hoogstade on the western front

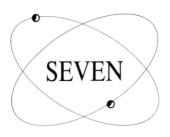

SEVEN

War Years

1914-1918

On June 28, 1914, Archduke Francis Ferdinand—heir to the throne of Austria-Hungary—was assassinated by a Serbian student. Austria-Hungary gained Germany's support, and then issued an ultimatum to Serbia. Austria-Hungary rejected Serbia's response and declared war on Serbia. On August 4, World War I began. Overnight, the war became very real to Irène and Ève at L'Arcouest. Aline Perrin's father was drafted and returned to Paris at once. Postal service became hit-or-miss, cutting the little fishing village off from the world.

Irène was ashamed of playing tennis and swimming at such a time. She wanted to participate in the war effort like some of her older friends. "I would dearly like to bring you back but it is impossible for the moment," Marie replied to Irène's incessant pleas. Several L'Arcouest fishers accused the two sisters of being German because they spoke a foreign language—Polish—to their cook and governess. So Irène started giving the two Polish women daily French lessons. She also took them to be photographed in order to get a permit allowing them to travel within France.

Marie genuinely missed her girls. In one of the few times on record, Marie showed her feelings for them: "I am dying to come and hug you. I don't have the time.... There are moments when I don't know what to do, I want to hold you close so badly." Lonesome as Irène was, she did not find it strange that her mother should insist on remaining in Paris. Irène was old enough to realize that, even though Mé wouldn't say so, she liked to hear from her daughters. So Irène wrote daily, even when she had nothing to say.

Marie foresaw terrible casualties because of the frightful new weapons. To her amazement, she discovered that few hospitals were aware of X rays, and none had the equipment to use them. The army health service was in even poorer shape. Marie had never personally worked with these rays. But she knew their use could facilitate the speedy location of metal fragments and broken bones in the wounded. And time could be an important factor in many cases. Marie requested a leave of absence from her university obligations to devote herself full-time to war work.

She assumed the directorship of the Red Cross's Radiological Service and, at the same time, agreed to establish X-ray installations where needed. Marie at once commandeered whatever X-ray apparatus she found in Paris to install in as many of the city's hospitals as possible. Marie realized that the wounded would not have to be transported far to get quick attention if specially equipped radiological cars were near the western front and at the base hospitals. A fleet of ordinary cars could be transformed to make up a crude but effective X-ray system. Only someone with Marie's prestige could undertake such a staggering endeavor. Extremely determined, she browbeat the unconvinced, overworked War Ministry into granting authorization to set up this mobile X-ray service.

By mid-September, Marie felt the war situation had stabilized. There was no indication that the war would be over soon, but Paris was no longer in immediate danger. So she sent for her daughters. But now that they could leave L'Arcouest, Irène was unable to. Three days earlier, while climbing on the cliffs along the shore, she had a bad fall. Her left foot was cut so badly it would be at least two weeks until the wound healed. Marie counseled patience and sent along, as a consolation, some more mathematics problems.

Early in October 1914, the girls returned to Paris. Nine-year-old Ève was packed off daily to primary school and learned to knit for the soldiers. Seventeen-year-old Irène entered the Sorbonne, majoring in mathematics and physics, and also enrolled in a nursing course. Marie was gone more than she was at home. Whenever Marie had the time, Irène hired a horse and buggy and helped her transfer materials

During the war, the radium was dissolved in water in a minute glass flask and put in a bomb-proof safe deposit box in the cellar of this small, detached building between the Curie and Pasteur pavilions, which was then surrounded with sandbags.

from the old laboratory to the Curie Institute. Irène had the responsibility of organizing and classifying the specimens of radioactive materials and hundreds of scientific journals in the new library.

Marie kept for herself a big, hand-cranked Renault with a truck body and a windshield, but no doors for the front seat. Fully equipped as a mobile X-ray system, "Radiological Car E's" maximum speed was a lumbering 20 miles per hour. Its color was the only thing that conformed to military specifications. It was painted army gray, with a Red Cross and a French flag on either side.

By the time Car E was ready, Irène had received sufficient training in her nursing class and from Marie to go along as part of her team. Thrilled to no longer be considered a child, Irène lived up to her mother's confidence. These first months together in the field tightened the bonds between Irène and Marie, who soon accepted Irène as an equal.

By November 1, 1914, there were 310,000 dead and 300,000 wounded on the French side alone. Seeing so many young men disfigured and crippled filled 17-year-old Irène with a lifelong horror of war.

The French soldiers affectionately nicknamed the 20-plus radiological cars Marie put in service *les Petites Curie,* the little Curies. The team of Car E consisted of Marie, Irène, a doctor, a military assistant, and a military chauffeur. On November 1, they set forth on their first field trip to the military hospital in Creil. From time to time, patrols stopped them. They were amazed to see Marie in her dusty brown coat, a round battered hat pulled down over her ears, an old leather briefcase alongside. Angrily, they demanded to know what a woman was doing out there. But after glancing at her papers, they quickly waved Car E on.

The radiological cars, called the Petites Curie, *in the courtyard of the Invalides—the veterans' home established by Louis XIV in the heart of Paris*

As soon as Car E arrived at the bomb-damaged building that served as the Creil field hospital, the surgeon came out to greet them. Unshaven, with drawn face and eyes blood-shot from lack of sleep, he was a non-believer where X rays were concerned. Without wasting a minute in idle conversation, Marie and Irène helped unload their cumbersome equipment. Irène showed the local nurses how to seal the room tight by blacking out the windows with curtains. Marie arranged their equipment. Because of ignorance about the danger of overexposure to radiation, cloth gloves, goggles, and a few metal screens were the only protective equipment used. Everyone present was warned to avoid the direct beam of the rays whenever possible. Nonetheless, Irène received massive doses of radiation.

Within half an hour of their arrival, the first bloody, muddy patient was wheeled in. One after another, the stretchers succeeded each other. A soldier wanted to know if it would hurt.

Marie replied encouragingly that it wouldn't hurt any more than having his picture taken.

From the beginning, Marie's greatest problems came from the military medical staff. Few if any of the doctors or surgeons had confidence in radiology. They resented the intrusion of civilian aid and, what was even worse, help from a woman. Like Marie, Irène was equal to whatever shocks and hardships, even dangers, each exhausting day offered. When the pair were in the field, they lived like soldiers—traveling in all kinds of weather, sleeping where they could, eating whatever was available. Through it all, the Curie Institute was never far from Marie's thoughts. She was continually filling her worn briefcase with envelopes of rosemary, fennel, and other seeds, picked here and there, to plant in the institute's garden when time and weather allowed.

Before too long, there were a number of hospitals near the western front where Marie set up permanent X-ray installations. Marie had no fixed schedule, never wore a special uniform or a nurse's veil. She worked bare-headed, dressed in an ordinary white laboratory coat. Whenever she received an alert about some malfunctioning equipment, Marie was off, adjusting a Red Cross armband and stuffing into her pocket her big wallet containing her military passes.

Irène accompanied Marie whenever possible. At the same time, she continued her Sorbonne studies as best she could. She and Ève attached a large map to the dining room wall to better follow the war and Mé's nomadic life. They stuck little flags on it to indicate the various places she had been.

The following fall, Marie did not hesitate to leave Irène in complete charge of the X-ray service in a hospital at Hoogstade, Belgium, a few kilometers from the western front. By now Marie knew Irène was capable of carrying on in her stead. The Belgian military doctor at Hoogstade, to whom Irène would teach the method of locating metal fragments with the X-ray equipment, was hard to handle. He was, she informed Marie, "the enemy of the most elementary notions of geometry." One poor soldier was wheeled in with a thigh bone crushed by a metal fragment. The doctor stubbornly refused to probe for the metal through the side from which Irène indicated it was accessible. He insisted upon entering through the gaping wound—and found nothing. Only then was he willing to heed Irène who, for a second time, suggested in her calm, serious voice that he explore the region indicated by the X rays. He did so and was able to extract the fragment at once.

When a call for help came from Amiens, Marie was busy elsewhere. So she once more substituted Irène. The Amiens military hospital was a big one. Unlike in Hoogstade, where an X-ray service was already established, here Irène had to start from scratch. Amiens had been occupied by the Germans and was more than half destroyed before it was finally liberated. The *Petite Curie* that drove Irène there had a hard time threading its way through the narrow, rubble-filled streets crowded with military transports.

Irène remained in Amiens a month and was late for the opening of the Sorbonne in the fall of 1916. After that she divided her time between classes at the Sorbonne and helping her mother set up a series of six-week training courses

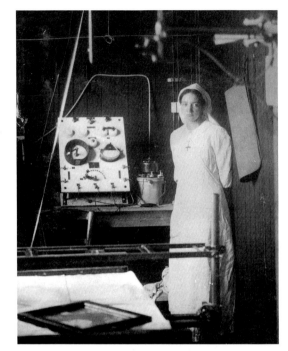

Irène in the X-ray room of the Amiens military hospital in 1916

at the Curie Institute. Marie decided this was the best way to remedy her own critical shortage of trained technicians and radiologists. Irène refused to let her supercharged schedule interfere with her Sorbonne studies. That summer, she received her *licence ès sciences physiques*. She was then appointed by the Sorbonne to serve as her mother's personal assistant in the university's laboratory.

On November 11, 1918, Germany agreed to sign a peace agreement. In the succeeding months, the U.S. Army paid $75 a week to have Marie train 20 officers in the use of X rays and radiological equipment at the Curie, while they awaited evacuation home. Irène handled their daily laboratory exercises. Any officer who used flattery to try and win the favor of the young woman was met with a cold stare.

Irène's long-sleeved, ankle-length, white smock, when the skirts of most girls her age had already crept up to the calf, typified her no-nonsense approach to her work.

This reserved Irène was not the Irène her friends knew. Most of her friends were L'Arcouest companions who had known her since childhood and attended the Cooperative with her. Irène was comfortable with them, and they with her. She wrote Marie that she had rearranged the furniture in the living room to leave a "respectable space for dancing," the current craze that was sweeping Paris.

With the war behind her, Marie officially inaugurated the Curie Pavilion of the Institut du Radium, the first laboratory she could truly call her own. To create the world-renowned school of radioactivity of her dreams, she must now assemble a staff and furnish the building with the latest equipment.

Irène and Marie trained these American officers to use X rays and radiological equipment.

Irène and Marie in the lab of the Institut du Radium in 1923

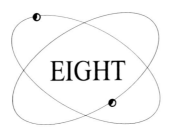

EIGHT

The Curie Pavilion

1918-1924

The postwar years were difficult for everyone in Europe, including Marie. At 52, Marie's sole support for herself and her two daughters was her small professor's salary from the Sorbonne, where she resumed teaching. This salary included her work as head of the Curie Pavilion. It was a great joy for Marie to have Irène in the laboratory with her. Irène was concentrating on the strenuous practical work required for her doctorate. Marie was concentrating, when in the laboratory, on isolating and purifying polonium. She was building as big a stockpile as possible of this radioactive element, because it was the best known source of the strong alpha rays essential for nuclear work.

In the 1920s, most physicists worldwide were not concerned with the atom's nucleus but with its husk, or outer covering. The Curie Institute, the Institut für Radiumforschung in Vienna, and the Cavendish Laboratories in Cambridge, England—headed by Marie's friend Ernest Rutherford—were the main centers in Europe devoted to the study of radioactivity and the atom's nucleus.

This period was one of great frustration for Marie. Because of an understaffed office, she wasted a lot of time typing replies to a never-ending flow of mail. Other precious hours were spent chasing after cheap war surplus to fill some of her laboratory's most urgent needs, and in similar small jobs that someone else could easily have done for her.

Marie rarely saw the press. Accordingly, she turned down a request for a personal interview by a visiting American journalist in mid-1920. But Missy Meloney was a match for Marie. As persistent as Marie and 14 years her junior, Mrs. Meloney's career was as unusual for a woman in her field as Mme Curie's was in hers. Unhampered by a slight limp and chronic ill health, Missy was the editor of a well-known women's magazine, the *Delineator.* She was in Europe to make a firsthand report on the generous contributions of the magazine's publishers to European war victims. Over the past 20 years she had interviewed an impressive list of international celebrities. She hoped to see Mme Curie.

The word "no" was not in Missy's vocabulary. Once she set out to do something, she was as determined as Marie. Undaunted by Marie's refusal to see her, she discovered, after considerable effort, a mutual acquaintance and tried again. Inexplicably Marie said yes. While Missy's French was adequate for the occasion, she quickly realized that Marie was proud of her smattering of English. Missy got off to a good start with Marie when she cannily conducted the interview in English.

Even with her hat on, the gray-haired journalist with the liquid black eyes only reached Marie's forehead. They met in Marie's bare office. Marie's unanticipated timidity made the veteran journalist ill at ease. She found herself apologizing for wasting Marie's valuable time. Missy quickly discovered that while America had about 50 grams of radium—Marie knew the location of each grain—France only had little more than a gram, and that was at the Curie. Missy was amazed. Marie had only a gram?

No, Marie corrected her. It wasn't hers. It was the laboratory's.

Impulsively, Missy asked: If Marie could have one thing in the entire world, what would it be?

That was an easy question for Marie. A gram of radium of course—for research.

Missy learned that the chief use for Marie's single gram was to provide radon, the gas milked from radium, for the treatment of cancer. Missy also found out that Marie's new laboratory was woefully short of essential equipment. Missy and Marie got along well together, and Marie invited her to visit at the Quai de Béthune apartment.

Missy had discovered a wonderful story. She foresaw no problem in finding enough generous American women to donate money to buy a gram of radium for Marie. But Mme Curie must come to the United States to accept their gift. Would she?

As Marie learned more about the petite American, her confidence in Missy grew and strengthened a budding friendship. A major factor influencing Marie's ultimate decision to go was the splendid travel opportunity the trip afforded her two daughters. This, plus the anticipated material gains for the Curie, far outweighed the terrifying publicity and tiring travel that Marie knew would be involved. Marie also wanted an appointment—incognito—with a leading American eye specialist. Her ears were buzzing continually, and her eyes had been growing steadily weaker. But it was only recently that she had admitted she was having trouble and learned she was facing a double cataract operation. For the first time, she voiced a suspicion that must have been gnawing at her for years. Could radium, her own child, be responsible?

Soon Marie boarded the westward bound SS *Olympic,* accompanied by her two girls and Missy Meloney. The president of the White Star Steamship Line was on hand to escort Marie to the bridal suite. She had not been in it 10 minutes before she examined the heating system and the way the furniture was fastened in place. The closet light fascinated Marie. It shone whenever the door was opened, but she could not locate the switch. When Marie failed to appear in the dining room at mealtime, someone was sent to fetch her. She found Marie sitting inside the wardrobe, in the dark, trying to figure out how the light functioned.

Missy had raised $150,000—a colossal sum for the day— to purchase Marie's radium. The money did not come from the rich alone. It also came from women in every walk of life who emptied their pockets for the Marie Curie Radium Fund. Marie's arrival was timed to coincide with the appearance on the New York newsstands of the April issue of the *Delineator.* The magazine was almost entirely devoted to Marie. Missy's lead article, "The Greatest Woman in the World," followed her editorial, "That Thousands Shall Not Die," and elaborated on the debt society owed "The Radium Woman" for discovering a cure for cancer.

So successfully had Missy emphasized Marie's scorn for monetary gain and her desire to serve humanity that she touched America's heart and purse strings. Missy transformed Marie into front-page news. For someone like Marie, who was so afraid of crowds, the sight of the exuberant, warm-hearted welcome awaiting her at the pier must have been appalling. There were thousands of cheering, waving people; groups of Girl Scouts; a 300-strong delegation from the Polish-American Society; blaring brass bands simultaneously playing the American, French, and Polish national

Ève, Marie, and Irène Curie, photographed upon their arrival in the United States

anthems. A horde of journalists and photographers clambered noisily on board the SS *Olympic,* armed with notepads and cameras. Missy hovered by protectively. On Marie's right stood carelessly dressed, earnest Irène. "Peasant-like" was an adjective many journalists applied to her. She was wearing sturdy, no-nonsense shoes and black stockings like her mother. In stark contrast, on her mother's left, was outgoing, perfectly poised Ève. Despite her meager budget, the younger sister managed to look like an elegant Parisian. Her eyes sparkled so mischievously that one of the press promptly dubbed her "Miss Radium Eyes."

To reach the door of the apartment placed at Marie's disposal, Marie had to wade through a sea of flowers. These were sent by a rose grower who had been cured of cancer by radium treatments. Marie had two days of official ceremonies in New York. Then she visited Smith, Vassar, and Mount Holyoke colleges for women, where she received honorary degrees. Not all American scientists, however, put themselves out on her account. Some agreed with certain distinguished European colleagues who maintained that, since Pierre's death, Mme Curie had done nothing of great importance in the laboratory. Harvard was one of the few major American universities in the East that would not award her an honorary degree.

By the time Marie, escorted by Vice President and Mrs. Calvin Coolidge, left New York, she carried her right arm in a sling—the result of too many handshakes from eager fans. When she arrived in Washington, D.C., it was late on the eve of the ceremonial presentation of the gram of radium.

Missy showed Marie the deed of the gift. Marie was aghast to learn that the radium was to be given to her, not to the Curie. Furthermore, no provisions were made concerning the gram's future. So long as Marie was alive, there was no problem. It would be used solely for scientific work. But what about after her death? Marie insisted that the document must spell out her wishes, then and there. The radium was to be an outright gift to her laboratory and only for scientific use. A new document was drawn up and translated into French so Marie could be sure that her wishes were being carried out. Then it was witnessed on the spot.

Marie appeared, the following afternoon, in the East Room of the White House, wearing the same black dress she had worn at both Nobel ceremonies. Over her slender neck, President Harding slipped a narrow ribbon from which hung a minuscule gold key. This key unlocked the heavy, lead-lined box especially designed for the radium that sat on a table nearby.

Marie with President Harding on the steps of the White House just after the presentation ceremony in 1921

Receptions followed at the French Embassy and the Polish Legation. Then came stops in Philadelphia and Pittsburgh. Limping more pronouncedly than ever, Missy drooped. Marie was exhausted. Back in New York, Marie collapsed. Missy's doctor ordered complete rest. Her tour schedule was revised accordingly, and most of the western part canceled. Various strategies were resorted to in order to spare Marie as many mob scenes as possible. Acting as her mother's proxy, Irène received numerous honorary degrees. Irène's English was adequate for her to deliver three speeches on radium that she had been requested to give—as Irène Curie, not as a stand-in for her mother.

Largely for her daughters' sakes, Marie insisted that the Grand Canyon remain on the itinerary. Even there, she was recognized and people gathered to stare. From Irène's point of view, visiting this wonder of nature was worth the whole trip. She and Ève went down on mule-back to the Colorado River at the bottom of the canyon, while Marie indulged in the purchase of a turquoise and silver Indian necklace—one of the very few pieces of jewelry she ever owned.

They returned east by way of Chicago and Buffalo, to see another tourist attraction, Niagara Falls. Marie took a childlike delight in the ride back into New York City in a cavalcade spearheaded by the city's motorcycle police, their sirens screeching. For Irène and Ève, the trip was a kaleido-scope of impressions geared more to their own age: a sing-along at one of the women's colleges; ice cream sodas at New York's Schrafft's; a brief visit to Coney Island. But the trip had taken its toll on Marie. An American physicist who knew her from international scientific meetings found her a distinctly "pathetic figure.... She seemed frightened at all the fuss people made over her."

Even so, the trip's success exceeded Marie's wildest dreams. The Curie Laboratory would now be the worthy equal of its most up-to-date foreign counterpart. Besides her gram of radium, she brought back $22,000 worth of meso-thorium and other precious minerals. There were gifts of equipment and numerous cash awards Marie received from different American scientific societies.

The trip also produced an intangible result that was perhaps more important than everything else combined. It taught Marie the power of American-style public relations. Marie realized she was her own best salesperson. She was no longer bashful about going around, hat in hand. She held a trump card. In the world of pure science, her fame as the discoverer of radium might rest on radium's potential as the key to unlock the structure of the universe. But for the general public, her fame rested—and still rests—on radium's ability to help in the fight against cancer. This was the one area of her scientific research that had any popular appeal. Everyone could relate to it.

Missy called Marie's work outside of the laboratory "dignifying science." Marie wanted to spare other young scientists, at the start of their careers, the hardships she and Pierre had experienced. So she lent a persuasive voice to pleas for scientific fellowships. She willingly accepted ceremonies and official trips as her professional obligation.

To recuperate after so much strenuous travel, Marie and the girls went off for a long vacation together at L'Arcouest. In September 1921, Marie left for Cavalaire to oversee a small house she was building on the Mediterranean. Ève returned to Paris to study for her *baccalauréat* examinations, and Irène stayed on. She was enjoying herself with her friends from the Cooperative days and had a pet raccoon that slept in her room and amused her immensely. An excellent athlete, she decided to take time off later that winter to resume skiing for the first time since the war.

Marie was ashamed of the thick glasses she now wore. To maintain the illusion that she still had perfect vision, she put color-coded signs on her instrument dials. She wrote her lecture notes in enormous block letters. Her staff played

Irène was one of the first women to ski in France. She took it up before World War I when she was 16.

along. To help keep the illusion at the dinner table, Irène and Ève passed the salt shaker to her the minute she started fumbling for it.

The effects of radioactivity on the human body were still far from being recognized. No one knew if the same radiation that was treating certain types of malignant cells so successfully might also have harmful effects on healthy cells. Then five colleagues who had worked with radium and thorium over the past two decades died, one after the other. These suspicious deaths were signs that Marie could no longer ignore. Radiation very likely was involved. In a report issued by the Curie Institute, the possibility of occupational hazards was acknowledged, and screens of lead and wood were declared effective against the rays.

Irène experienced a tremendous sense of fulfillment working in the laboratory. She was fascinated with the rapidly developing study of the atom's nucleus and had already embarked on the study of polonium that was to be her lifework. There was no better radiochemist than Marie to teach Irène the difficult, delicate task of preparing and purifying polonium for her experiments. Meticulous care, ingenuity, and sometimes speed were necessary. She learned how to bombard a screen of matter with alpha rays and to study the bombardment's results through a microscope. An article on the speed of the alpha rays of polonium—in the French Academy's *Comptes Rendus*—marked the debut of Irène's research of the properties of polonium. The completed research would constitute her doctoral thesis.

Irène and Marie in the laboratory, using Pierre's piezo-quartz electrometer, in 1923

At this time, the French legislature finally decided to support scientific research for its own sake, outside of the realm of teaching. The Curie Institute was one of the first beneficiaries of this new government spending. Marie allocated one-fifth of the small sum it received to support Irène's experiments. This was not the first—and would not be the last—time that Marie showed favoritism at the Curie where her older daughter was concerned. Some of the staff grumbled. While Irène's competence was already proven, she had a prickly disposition. She did not exude charm or warmth. She carried her father's indifference to people one step further and did not hide her opinion when she considered present company to be unwelcome. Colleagues often witnessed Irène's disconcerting habit of reaching under her laboratory smock and lifting up her skirt to pull a soiled handkerchief from a petticoat pocket and loudly blow her nose. This amazing performance caused more than one intruder to stop mid-sentence and retreat. Curtness was Irène's long suit. Aside from childhood friends and family, few ever got to know her well, especially at the Curie, where the "Crown Princess of Science" ruffled more feathers than she bothered to smooth.

The Curie Foundation celebrated the 25th anniversary of the discovery of radium in December 1923. Marie's sisters and brother, civil and military authorities, and delegations from the French legislature and the great schools were all present in the Sorbonne's amphitheater. The president of France presided, and the rector of the Université de Paris spoke. Later Irène demonstrated some of her parents' earliest experiments. The government officially thanked Marie for her many contributions to science by awarding her an annual pension. This monetary gesture had been done only

The Curie Pavilion of the Institut du Radium. To the left is the tiny amphitheater where Marie gave lectures to her students and behind the Curie, to the right, is the Pasteur Pavilion.

once before — with Pasteur. Moreover, the pension was to be passed on to Irène and Ève on Marie's death.

One day, a month or two later, Irène caught a brief glimpse of a young lieutenant in a blue officer's uniform leaving her mother's office. The next time Irène saw him was almost a year later at the very end of December 1924, when he rang the bell at #36 Quai de Béthune, and she answered the door. He apologized for intruding and explained that he had made a special trip to deliver a letter requested by Marie.

"One minute, Monsieur," Irène replied. Without giving him a second glance, or so much as telling him to enter, she disappeared, leaving him to stand hesitantly at the open door.

*Fred and Irène at the Tennis Club about the time of their marriage.
Fred was a fiend about playing tennis and would have a court built
as soon as they built their own home some years later in the Paris
suburbs. He always had to win.*

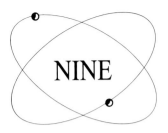

NINE

Irène Joliot-Curie
1924-1926

Frédéric Joliot was born on March 19, 1900, in a comfortable middle-class home in Paris. As a boy, Fred was fascinated with the stories he read about Pasteur and the Curies. He cut Marie and Pierre's pictures out of a popular magazine and hung them in the place of honor in his makeshift chemistry laboratory, which he rigged up in the family bathroom. And more than once, when his mother went to wash the supper dishes in the kitchen, she could not use the water because Fred had some mysterious apparatus attached to the faucet. She recorded in her diary: "Fred has gone mad. He invents some oil lamps and dirties... everything."

When the time came for higher education, Fred enrolled, for financial reasons, in Paris' tuition-free EPCI. EPCI was hallowed ground for him because of its close associations with his childhood heroes—the Curies. The school's director of studies, Paul Langevin, a close friend of both Marie and Pierre, was the first to recognize Fred's enormous potential.

After Fred finished at EPCI and his required military service was ending, he was more interested in doing basic research than in going into industry. So Langevin, knowing that Marie had an opening, recommended Fred to her.

Fred's feelings can be imagined when, still in uniform, he was ushered into Marie's office at the Curie on November

21, 1924. There before him at her desk sat his childhood hero. She was much smaller than he expected, but she looked exactly like she did in the faded magazine picture that still hung on his wall. He never guessed that they might meet one day. It was not easy for him to talk with Mme Curie. As usual, Marie's own shyness made her even more unapproachable.

Soon after, Fred reported for work. Irène was in the midst of an experiment when Fred was being shown around.

Fred, as a child, is learning to play the French hunting horn in June 1906. His father, Henri Joliot, taught and composed tunes for the instrument.

She barely raised her head to acknowledge their introduction. Three years younger than Irène, Fred had fine, clean-cut features. His laughter echoed often in the Curie's normally silent halls. He quickly made friends with his coworkers. His friendliness and charm appealed equally to men and women and thawed even the shyest of the foreign students at the Curie. In that formal atmosphere, where everyone was Mademoiselle, Madame, or Monsieur no matter how long they worked together, he was quickly known as Fred to one and all.

Marie was not long in coming to appreciate Fred's exceptional qualities and great drive. But she would never accept the perpetual cigarette hanging from his lip. She promptly specified that smoking was only allowed in one laboratory in the sub-basement—where she rarely ventured —or outdoors.

Since Fred knew little about working with radioactive material, Marie turned him over to Irène. Irène was to teach him the techniques Marie and Pierre had pioneered. She also was to familiarize him with the various apparatus there, many of which he had never seen in operation.

Irène being Irène, it is questionable if she paid much attention, at first, to her dashing new coworker. Not that Irène was averse to male company. She enjoyed attending dances and, that March, stayed at one till 8:00 A.M., "which is a record," she wrote Marie. But when Irène was at the Curie, she was there to work. She had never seen the need for useless conversation and considered the customary social niceties a waste of time. Irène often did not even say "hello" to anyone when she arrived in the morning. Preoccupied with the day's experiment she was about to set up, she hurried in, slipped on her long, white, acid-stained smock and rushed to her laboratory bench. Many others in the laboratory were taken aback by her imperturbable calm, which they mistook for coldness. Her direct manner in answering questions was mistaken for haughtiness.

In fairness to Irène, her position as both daughter and personal assistant of *la patronne*—as Marie was known at the Curie—was not an easy one. Colleagues often failed to give Irène's ability its due. Once Fred startled her with the question: What was it like to be the daughter of famous parents? After a moment's reflection, Irène replied, "Fame was something from the outside. It really had no connection with us." Unlike most children who choose to follow in the steps of celebrated parents, Irène was neither intimidated nor discouraged by Pierre and Marie's fame.

The next year was a tough, busy one for Fred. Intensely ambitious, he realized how much catching up he had to do—fast. Fred at first thought Irène lived only for the laboratory. Slowly, as they worked together each day, he was surprised to find that she enjoyed a good time as well as anybody and had a delightful sense of humor. Irène soon discovered that this cheerful, attractive newcomer shared her love of sports—long hikes in the mountains, skiing, swimming, tennis. Occasionally, if Fred had questions and there was no time to ask them at the laboratory, he waited outside at the end of the day. Then he walked home with Irène across the Pont de la Tournelle—the bridge over the Seine—to the Quai de Béthune in the quiet haven of the Île St. Louis. Gradually this walk turned into a nightly routine. They enjoyed each other's company, and before long their walks lengthened into excursions on the weekends to the woods around Paris.

In March 1925, Irène defended her doctoral thesis, "Research on the Alpha Rays of Polonium," in the Sorbonne's packed amphitheater. Unlike Marie, she did not suffer agonies when speaking before so large a group. Her self-confident voice rang out clearly. Marie was not present. The day belonged to Irène, and Marie did not wish to detract attention from her daughter by putting in an appearance.

Afterward Marie welcomed Irène and the entire staff at the institute to tea in the small garden between the Curie and Pasteur pavilions. These affairs were Marie's traditional way of celebrating whenever a member of her staff or family was awarded a hard-won degree or received a special prize. Because it was unseasonably warm, tables were set up under the budding lime trees and chairs were moved outside. Developing trays from the photographic darkroom were filled with cookies. Tea was made in laboratory flasks over Bunsen burners, and the laboratory beakers and glass stirring rods did double duty as teacups and spoons.

A young reporter appeared from *Le Quotidien*, a Paris daily, for an interview. She asked if Irène had chosen too punishing a career for a woman.

"Not at all," Irène replied. "I believe that men's and women's scientific aptitudes are exactly the same."

What about family obligations?

"These are possible on condition that they are accepted as additional burdens. For my part, I consider science to be the paramount interest of my life."

Was there any danger with radium?

Irène admitted she already had a radium burn, but it was not serious. Like her mother, she had periodic blood tests, which showed nothing abnormal.

Some time after her abrupt dismissal of the correspondent's question about family obligations as "additional burdens," Irène's relations with Fred turned serious. Early in

Irène in 1926 at the time she was married

1926, Irène appeared, as usual, with the breakfast she made for her mother and herself and sat down on the foot of Marie's bed. Before discussing the day's laboratory schedule, she casually broke the news of her engagement.

According to Ève, Marie could not have been more astonished. Earlier Marie had agreed to present a series of lectures in Rio de Janeiro in the interest of better Franco-Brazilian relations. And Irène—before she was engaged—had promised to accompany her. Marie saw no reason for any change of plans.

The trip itself took two weeks each way. Distance made correspondence erratic. Irène was not the first person to worry that the absence of mail meant a loss of interest on her fiancé's part. Unfortunately, when Fred's letters did arrive, Irène had a terrible time reading them. Gently, she poked fun at him with a personal deciphering manual:

Letters written in the hieroglyphic language invented in the 20th century by M. Frédéric Joliot, with their translation:

ι	α	ω
=	=	=
c, r, i, e, l, t	u, n	m

Furnished with these explanations, decipher as an exercise.

[Warning: A word is sometimes cut in two but, in general, two different words are not joined together, according to the Frédéric Joliot rules of penmanship.]

In her letters, Irène reveals the warm, frequently humorous, side of her nature. She missed Fred dreadfully. She worried about him. "You haven't told me whether you were smoking a reasonable or an unreasonable amount.... Try not to smoke like a factory smokestack, go 100 km an hour on your motorbike, and do all the other unreasonable things you are capable of."

Irène and Fred's marriage took place, privately, on October 9, 1926, in a civil ceremony. It was followed by a bridal lunch at the Quai de Béthune. Ève, who cared more about these details than her sister, took pains to see that the meal was properly festive. Then the bride and groom returned to their laboratory benches. With a total disregard for anything so conventional as spending their wedding night together, Fred went home to Montparnasse, and Irène, back to the Quai de Béthune. The next morning, Fred arrived with a single suitcase at the Curies', and the newlyweds saw Marie off to Copenhagen. She was to be away a week and was leaving the apartment at their disposal.

Irène and Fred at a Bastille Day festival in the fishing village of L'Arcouest, where they and other Sorbonne families had summer cottages

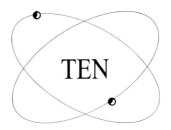

TEN

The Second Generation to the Fore

1927-1934

Early in the spring of 1927, Irène and Fred went south to the Mediterranean for a rest. Irène already had a foretaste of what it was like to be a "fisherman's widow." Some husbands, especially newly married ones, carry a picture of their bride around with them. But not Fred. "Ask him to show you the snap he carries in his wallet," Irène challenged a friend. The friend asked, and Fred obliged, producing a photo of a majestic pike, the largest one he ever caught.

Soon after they returned, Irène and Fred moved into an apartment of their own. It was in an unimposing, six-story building, which Marie bought as an investment with other *l'arcouestiens*, and was within comfortable walking distance of the Curie. There were two apartments to a floor, and theirs was on the fifth. Because they were always in a hurry, the pair preferred to race up and down the narrow winding stairs rather than trust the temperamental, rickety cage elevator.

Fred and Irène came to the Quai de Béthune for lunch —the mainstay of every French family—three or four times a week. Heated discussions raced back and forth between Fred and Marie so rapidly that an amused Irène could not get a word in and was reduced to the sidelines.

Irène was soon pregnant, but she worked right up until noon on September 17, 1927, when her daughter, Hélène, was born. Not long after, Irène was back at work. Every afternoon, the maid took Hélène to the Luxembourg Gardens, and whenever Marie was in Paris, she would appear at the same place. She devoted 30 minutes to the baby. Then, when the clock struck the hour, she kissed little Hélène good-bye, and returned to the laboratory and Irène and Fred.

Marie now limited herself to selecting and delegating the research projects of her new Sorbonne students. Irène was in charge of them. Fred was slowly working toward his doctorate while teaching a class at a private school and honing his research techniques at the Curie. By intense study, Fred was catching up with Irène. "The boy's a skyrocket," Marie declared with obvious pleasure, one day.

There were still only 300 grams of radium available in the entire world, and Marie was anxious to procure one for the new Marie Sklodowska-Curie Institute in Warsaw. The institute was nearing completion and lacked the money to buy radium. When Missy Meloney came through Paris in early 1929, Marie hurried to consult with her. Missy thought it would be possible to raise the money, if Marie would again travel to the United States.

Marie agreed to a far shorter trip than before and proved much fussier about details. Under Ève's gentle goading, she indulged in one new dress, with which Irène hoped she would "dazzle" everyone. She set sail in October. Marie spent the night at the White House as the guest of President and Mrs. Hoover, an unheard-of honor. She went to Dearborn, Michigan, to visit Henry Ford and attended his dinner in honor of another scientist, Thomas Edison. She also stayed in Schenectady, New York, with the head of General Electric, a company that donated lavishly to the Curie. Marie was now a professional at the art of discreet begging and had learned to enjoy the red-carpet treatment accorded her.

Most radioactive substances, while distinct elements, were available in only the smallest quantities. Many of their chemical properties had yet to be determined and described. This was a fertile field for study. Polonium's emission of abundant, matter-penetrating alpha particles made it easy to identify and track, especially as it produced almost no other type of radiation. So polonium was invaluable to researchers. Unquestionably, the direction of Fred and Irène's joint work was influenced by the availability of Marie's stockpile of polonium. And Marie, who had the final say as to who did what with this precious hoard, put it all at Irène and Fred's disposal. No longer did she dole it out, as in the past, in bits and pieces, to different researchers in the laboratory for various projects. Marie was a proud mother, and no one dared accuse *la patronne* of favoritism to her face.

Whenever they could find the time, Fred and Irène kept adding to this supply of polonium by complex radiochemistry. A laborious and highly technical task, it was also extremely dangerous, because of the high levels of radioactivity in the solutions they were handling. An adequate supply of polonium was essential if Irène and Fred were to make important discoveries in radioactivity. Some radioactive phenomena occurred rarely. So experiments had to be repeated over and over in order that these phenomena could be observed systematically.

The Wilson Cloud Chamber was Irène and Fred's favorite piece of equipment. The chamber gave them a direct,

Fred and Irène in the laboratory at the Curie in 1935

detailed view of the telltale tracks made by the jumble of particles released in a bombardment. These tracks provided invaluable information on the different types of particles producing them. The tracks only lasted a fraction of a second. Fred's innovative adaptation of the chamber enabled him to take pictures of the tracks for in-depth study. This made the chamber an invaluable tool with which to study the radioactive process.

Several more preliminaries in the exploration of the nucleus of the atom remained to be resolved. And only a handful of important scientists and a few hundred adventuresome, imaginative researchers were working on them. In 1930 this small world was startled and puzzled by the strange results of an experiment with polonium by a pair of German scientists, Walther Bothe and Herbert Becker.

The Germans' experiment was fairly common at that stage of nuclear physics. A radioactive substance was placed next to a non-radioactive one to try and deduce what happened as individual particles from the radioactive substance bombarded the non-radioactive one. The radiation could be studied either by measurement of its intensity or by photographs.

By the end of 1931, Irène and Fred had prepared the largest and most powerful source of pure polonium to date. There was just enough powdered polonium, when mounted on minuscule holders, to cover the bottom of a laboratory vial. Now the pair were ready to attempt to verify Bothe and Becker's mysterious phenomenon, which had intrigued them ever since its discovery. Irène and Fred bombarded a plate of beryllium with polonium. To their amazement, after a series of trials and errors, they seemed to have discovered a new fundamental characteristic of the Germans' radiation.

When he read the Joliot-Curie's report, "The Emission of Protons of Great Speed . . . Under the Influence of Gamma Rays," Marie's old friend Ernest Rutherford burst out impatiently, "I don't believe it." Believing that a particle as heavy as a proton could not be so easily moved, he asked his assistant at the Cavendish, James Chadwick, to investigate. Chadwick immediately went to work, convinced that Fred and Irène had discovered something "quite new as well as strange." Working around the clock and averaging only three hours of sleep nightly over a 10-day period, Chadwick discovered the neutron—the third elementary, subatomic particle. The other two were the proton—the hydrogen nucleus—and the electron—the electrically charged particle.

Chadwick's momentous discovery of the neutron, for which he later won the Nobel, occurred only seven weeks after Irène and Fred's report. Their work, in turn, had been based on Bothe and Becker's. Irène and Fred's chagrin when they learned of Chadwick's results can be easily imagined. How close they had come to discovering the neutron themselves!

Nuclear research was, as Chadwick put it, "simply a kind of sport. It was contending with nature." It was like solving a puzzle in which the difficulties of interpretation were accumulating faster than new knowledge could resolve them.

During the next seven years, until the outbreak of World War II, great breakthroughs would be made in nuclear physics. These breakthroughs would transform nuclear physics from a pure laboratory science to the atomic age of nuclear power engineering and nuclear weapons. In 1932 alone, five major discoveries were made, and Irène and Fred played a varying role in each one. Experiment followed experiment in rapid succession.

Marie, now in her 60s, had her fourth cataract operation. She rarely published any reports nowadays, but she still continued to lecture at 3:00 P.M. on Mondays and Wednesdays. The reluctant, gradual handing over of the reins at the Curie was in process. This was a difficult transition, eased somewhat by the knowledge that direction would ultimately remain in the family. Marie was present at a meeting of the venerable French Physics Society when Irène and

Fred gave an outstanding demonstration of their own experimental techniques and acute powers of observation. Marie confided, delightedly, to an old colleague who was walking her home afterward, that early spring night: "Doesn't this remind you of *la belle epoque* [the peak days] of our old laboratory!" She was reliving the thrill of those first early discoveries with Pierre.

Marie was not well. She had slipped in the laboratory and broken her right wrist. It was only a simple fracture that should have healed quickly, but it triggered a host of other ailments. Dizzy, weak, and slightly feverish, Marie was confined to bed for days on end. The maddening drumming in

Irène, Marie, and Hélène in 1930. About this time, Einstein saw the "particle tracks" that Hélène, already alert to the conversations around her, had scrawled on a sheet of paper. He warned, "if you don't watch out she'll become a theoretical physicist!" And she did.

her ears returned, the radium-induced sores on her fingers were festering, and she had a recurrence of her old gall-bladder problems. Although she was tired all the time, she continued working on a new textbook on radioactivity. At 8:45 every morning, her little Ford stopped on the quai in front of her apartment. The driver gave three honks, Marie flung on her hat and coat, and she was off to the Curie.

Irène herself was far from well. She had never fully recovered her strength after the birth of Hélène. She suffered increasing ill health and had adopted the attitude that if she ignored her aches and pains they would go away. As with the birth of Hélène, Irène was at her bench at the Curie until only a few hours before the birth of her second child. Pierre was born on March 12, 1932.

As Fred explained in a letter to a friend: "We have been working very hard. . . . We had to speed up the pace of our experiments for it is annoying to be overtaken by other laboratories which immediately take up one's experiments . . . as was done in Cambridge." Consequently Irène, who had contracted a painful case of pleurisy and was dreadfully thin, was back at the laboratory sooner than she should have been. The end of July found her returning to a sanatorium high in the Alps where she had already spent several brief stays in the past two years. Here tuberculosis was diagnosed. Fred managed as best he could alone in Paris, keeping an eye on his family, the household, and the laboratory—roles that he would assume more and more with the passage of time.

In 1933, Irène and Fred were flattered by an invitation to give a report on their latest work at the annual Solvay conference in Brussels. The conference was devoted, this year, to the structure and properties of the nucleus of the atom. Nuclear physicists were still a relatively small group. Among the 40-plus present were 6 Nobel laureates and 14 soon to be crowned. Fourteen countries and two generations were represented. Some, like Marie, Paul Langevin, and Jean Perrin, had attended the first Solvay conference 22 years earlier.

Even her critical sister Ève would have considered Irène, in her jumper and striped, short-sleeved blouse, the most stylish woman at the Solvay. Granted there were only two others: Marie was in her usual somber gown, and Lise Meitner, a slight, 55-year-old Austrian physicist, appeared in nondescript attire. Fred's clean-shaven face, almost the only one in the room, made him appear even younger. He gave their joint report. He would always do so, at Irène's request. Today marked their debut in these exalted spheres, and he, for once, was noticeably nervous.

Instead of their paper about their neutron findings being received with praise, a stormy controversy arose. An English physicist voiced a different interpretation of their results. He remained unconvinced even after Irène took the floor and tried to prove him wrong. Then Lise Meitner spoke up. Fräulein Meitner, whom Einstein would call "the German Marie Curie," was the head of the physics department at the magnificently equipped Kaiser Wilhelm Institute in Berlin. A formidable researcher, she was highly esteemed for hard, careful work and was always listened to with respect. She did not mince words. She and her colleagues had performed experiments similar to those of Irène and Fred. Never had they gotten the same results.

Everyone turned to look at Marie and her children. Bedlam broke out in that sedate gathering as everyone started arguing at once. Marie, who had listened to Fred's report so proudly, bristled but did not say a word. Irène and Fred stared at each other stupefied. To have the renowned Lise

Meitner disagree with them so emphatically at their first international conference was a catastrophe. And she had done it in front of tall, birdlike Chadwick, too, who had vaulted over their shoulders to the neutron's discovery.

The session was soon over. Marie stayed behind to talk to several people, and Irène and Fred wandered into the gardens. They were devastated. It was one thing for their basic hypothesis to be questioned. It was something else again to have the accuracy of their work doubted. They themselves knew that they had made no mistake. They always rechecked results carefully. The other delegates stood around admiring the flowers and talking in little groups to avoid the pair. It was evident from the way they averted their eyes that most felt confident that Lise Meitner was correct and the Joliot-Curies had been inaccurate. Hushed voices murmured that the young French couple were probably

The Solvay conference in Brussels in October 1933. Among those pictured are Irène Joliot-Curie, Marie Curie, and Lise Meitner.

working too fast. Since they had barely missed out on the discovery of the neutron, they were probably in a hurry to discover something else. They would not have wanted anybody to beat them to it.

The great Danish physicist Niels Bohr immediately realized that, if Irène and Fred were correct, the nucleus of the atom was far more complex than currently envisioned. Theories about it would need modification. Physically imposing with an enormous domed head, a long heavy jaw, and big hands, Bohr was one of the few to approach the couple that late afternoon. "What you are doing is of the greatest importance," he comforted in such a low voice they had to strain to hear him.

The next day, Chadwick was delighted to find his place at lunch was next to Marie's. As he sat down, she greeted him coldly, turned away, and completely ignored him for the entire meal. The snubbed Englishman consoled himself with the observation that the ailing woman seemed to lack sufficient energy to eat her meal, much less to indulge in any conversation. Others present were surprised to realize that even a national monument like Marie Curie had feelings where her immediate family were concerned. Irène and Fred remained subdued on the train back to Paris with Marie and the other French delegates.

In retrospect, Irène and Fred's Solvay fiasco produced some good. Their experiment was so scathingly denounced that no one took the trouble to investigate their claims. This left the pair temporarily without any competition. Still smarting from their humiliating experience, but stimulated by Bohr's encouragement, they immediately re-verified their controversial finding that neutrons had been emitted. The next step was to decide upon, and set up, an exhaustive series of experiments to determine the correct way to interpret the finding. They first ran a battery of tests using a Wilson Cloud Chamber and studied its photographs in great detail. Then they switched to a different set of experiments to determine the intensity of the rays they were getting. For this they used the latest model Geiger counter.

On Thursday afternoon, January 11, 1934, Fred was alone in the basement at the Curie. He bombarded his aluminum target with alpha rays from polonium and then slowly withdrew the polonium. The clatter of the counter, which indicated that particles were being emitted, did not die down at once, as it should have when the polonium was removed. "Top-top-top," the Geiger went right on counting—for a few more minutes. Fred was puzzled. What was happening? Not trusting his ears, he repeated the experiment. "Top-top-top," the Geiger continued as before. Once more it did not die abruptly, but gradually. What Fred was hearing now must be the sound of another, different radioactive particle. Barely able to contain his excitement, he rushed up the stairs, two at a time, to fetch Irène. She was on the second floor, working on a related chemical problem.

Fred reran the experiment without a word of explanation. Irène did not need one. Like Fred, she immediately recognized the importance of the sustained sound. Together, they reviewed what had occurred. Was the counter malfunctioning? The Geiger was a temperamental, delicate instrument—seeming to have a mind of its own.

Unfortunately, Irène and Fred had a dinner engagement they could not break. Before leaving, Fred called a friend down to the basement. Without telling him why, Fred asked him to check out the instrument and make sure it was functioning correctly. If the Geiger counter received a clean bill of health, Irène and Fred must have a detailed report ready for the French Academy's regular Monday meeting, three days later. Only then could they claim credit for their amazing discovery of an entirely new reaction. Radioactive material could be produced in a laboratory.

Their friend confirmed that there was nothing wrong with the Geiger counter. All Friday, January 12, and Saturday, January 13, the couple remained glued to their benches —Irène upstairs and Fred downstairs. Around 7:00 P.M. on Saturday, Fred heard footsteps in the corridor. It was one of the researchers with his hat and coat on, taking a shortcut through the underground passage from the annex to avoid a sudden downpour. When he saw Fred, he stopped to say good night. Fred had arrived at a point where he needed a third party to repeat the experiment and see if there were any flaws. Without disclosing any details, Fred asked the researcher to run a check on it, while he took a needed break for a smoke. The man confirmed Fred's results.

Some time that weekend, Irène and Fred invited Marie down. They also asked Paul Langevin. Fred briefed them. Then he and Irène presented their new experiment. Few words were spoken, except for a couple of questions and answers. Their hurriedly written, historic report, "A New Type of Radioactivity," was presented to the French Academy on schedule the following Monday, an incredible four days after Fred's initial observation.

Their report in the *Comptes Rendus* staked out Irène and Fred's claim. Now they must provide physical and visual proofs of the creation of this new radioelement out of aluminum—an isotope of phosphorus that is never found in nature because it is too unstable. This new radioelement, which lasted a little longer than three minutes before it decayed into

Paul Langevin (left) *gives Fred his sword as a new member of the French Academy — one of the highest honors in France. Langevin was one of Pierre's first students, and his grandson would later marry Hélène Joliot.*

another element, could only be detected by the tick of a Geiger counter. So they would have three minutes in which to work. When they met a fellow chemist on the rue Pierre Curie one day and stopped to ask for advice, he threw up his hands in amazement. He had never heard of having to function within such a brief time frame.

Only a master team could accomplish what the couple did. Their preparations were carefully worked out in advance. One morning, Fred bombarded the aluminum and stoppered the irradiated metal in a vial. Then Irène took over, employing every trick of radiochemistry that Marie had taught her. Fred reacted to her success like a child, running and jumping around in the empty basement laboratory.

Both of them got enormous satisfaction from the fact that their initial observations, given in their earlier Solvay report, had now been shown to be correct. The agonizing work entailed must have been worth it, from Irène's point of view, the day she and Fred gave Marie a sample of the first radioelement made in a laboratory. To verify its contents, Marie took the tiny vial in her scarred, radium-damaged fingers and held it near a Geiger counter. They never forgot the intense joy in her face as she heard the instrument's telltale chatter—"top-top-top."

The lifework of two generations of the Curie family dovetailed. The parents discovered natural radioactivity, which was the property of a few elements, and their study of it led to the penetration of the atom's structure. Their daughter and son-in-law discovered an entirely different reaction: how people could duplicate radioactivity by artificial means.

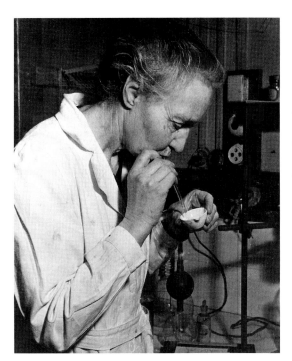

Irène, in her lab, transfers minute amounts of radioactive substances with a pipette

Marie on the porch of her laboratory at the Institut du Radium. She is looking over the tiny garden between the Curie and Pasteur pavilions.

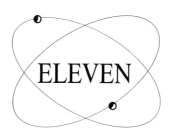

ELEVEN

The Curtain Falls

1934

Irène and Fred might be the French spearheads in this attack to lay bare the inner workings of the atom. But scientists in Copenhagen, Göttingen, Rome, Berlin, Cambridge, and the United States were soon competing in the race that would lead to the liberation of atomic energy. Irène and Fred continued to come regularly to the quiet Quai de Béthune for lunch and kept Marie abreast of the world outside as well as inside the Curie. Turbulence was beginning all over Europe. Hitler had come to power in Germany in January 1933, and the next month the Nazi persecution of the Jews commenced. The Curie family friend, Albert Einstein, was invited to accept a chair at the Collège de France in Paris, but the Institute for Advanced Study in Princeton won out.

The family's efforts to get Marie, at age 67, to slow down and take better care of herself were exercises in futility. Because research on actinium was not progressing fast enough to suit her, Marie lent a hand. Separating pure actinium X was a tedious, slow job. She worked at her bench straight through the dinner hour and was still there at 2:00 in the morning. One final operation remained. Marie stayed seated alongside the noisy, clanking centrifuge for another hour. Nothing else in the world existed for her except the whirling liquid. When the experiment was finished, and she did not get the hoped-for result, she slumped in her chair. The picture of despondency with her arms crossed, her gaze empty, she sadly admitted failure.

Marie did not trudge around the Curie as much as she used to. But Irène always knew when she managed to make it down to the basement room where the Wilson Cloud Chambers were kept. Those days chain-smoker Fred invariably came home with a telltale cigarette burn in his shirt pocket. Marie's rules still forbade smoking on the premises. So whenever Fred heard her familiar footsteps, he stuffed the forbidden cigarette out of sight in the first place available.

Marie's health continued its slow descent. Stumped for an answer when called in for consultation, four of the most

Irène with Albert Einstein — a longtime family friend of the Curies — at Princeton, where Einstein worked at the Fuld Institute for Advanced Study

Marie, Irène holding up Pierre, Hélène, Fred, and Mme Joliot at a family gathering—about 1933

distinguished doctors in Paris recommended an immediate departure for a sanatorium in the mountains to conquer her lingering fever. There Marie took a sudden turn for the worse. She was now even too weak to enjoy the splendid vista of Mont Blanc from her private verandah. A renowned specialist from Geneva recognized extreme pernicious anemia and held out no hope.

On July 4, 1934, with Irène, Fred, and Ève by her side, Marie Curie died. She was a victim of years of overexposure to radiation. Her own child, radium, was the villain.

Five days later, Ève sent Missy Marie's watch, which had once belonged to Pierre, with a little note: "It has no value except that she wore it always and liked it. It was on her table near her bed when she died."

Fred (far right) *and Irène receive the Nobel Prize from King Gustav V at the official Nobel ceremonies in Stockholm, Sweden. Gustav V awarded the Nobel twice to Irène's mother and once to her father—a family accomplishment never since equalled.*

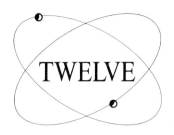

TWELVE

Irène Carries On

1934-1958

It was a foregone conclusion in international scientific circles that, as Marie had predicted, Irène and Fred would receive a Nobel for their synthesis of new radioelements. So they could not have been too surprised, in November 1935, when the wire came from Stockholm. Irène clearly recalled the arrival of the press when her parents received a similar telegram. To avoid a similar onslaught, she hustled Fred off to get lost in the crowds at a big department store not far from the Curie—and bought a needed plastic tablecloth. The next day at the Curie, at the traditional tea to celebrate a staff worker's success, Irène was congratulated on all sides. Artlessly she replied: "In our family we are accustomed to glory." Coming from her this was not boastful. It was a statement of fact.

The repercussions of the Nobel award with its attendant obligations marked even more of a turning point in Fred and Irène's lives than it had in Marie and Pierre's. Both were already well aware of their responsibilities as scientists in a world of change. "Disinterested" no longer ranked high in the vocabulary of Irène's generation of scientists. "Responsibility" was their theme song. And now with their growing worldwide acclaim, there were ever-increasing demands on the couple's time.

The family had long since outgrown their crowded apartment. When the house they were building in the Paris suburb of Antony, adjoining Sceaux, was finished, Irène was once more away in a sanatorium. So Fred moved the children into the house. Their new home was unpretentious, but there were separate studies for Fred and Irène, as well as ample ground for a tennis court for Fred and for Irène's flowers. Antony was within easy commuting distance from the Curie and the Sorbonne. Equally important, there was a good school for Hélène and Pierre, recently renamed "Marie Curie," at Sceaux.

When Irène's doctors permitted her to come home, they cautioned that she resume work "in moderation," a phrase that was not in her vocabulary. She was so anxious to get back to the laboratory, even if she was supposed to rest each afternoon, that a cot was moved into her office at the Curie. Some 15 nationalities were represented there now and included several women. A point would always be made to retain approximately this same mix of researchers—exactly as during Marie's lifetime.

On a cold morning, Irène could once more be found standing in front of the radiator in the vestibule next to the main entry, her acid-stained white laboratory coat and skirt lifted high to warm her rear. The vestibule was a convenient, popular focal point for conversation, and with several students and researchers seated alongside, Irène fielded technical questions. She was not averse to a quick discussion of some of the day's burning problems. Like Fred—and unlike Marie—Irène was determined to speak out on nonscientific matters when she felt strongly about the issues at stake.

Irène believed that the government must guarantee equal working conditions for both men and women, and she

Fred and Irène — with Pierre in the background — at L'Arcouest in 1938. Fred was more at ease with the fishermen at L'Arcouest than he was in scientific circles.

wanted all women to join in a common fight for civil, as well as for political, rights. Women still did not have the right to vote in France, but Léon Blum, the president of the council, was anxious to bring women into the government for the first time. When he asked Irène to be one of the three to enter his cabinet as undersecretaries in their respective fields, she agreed to serve—briefly. As she explained to Missy, "Fred and I thought I must accept it as a sacrifice for the feminist cause in France, although it annoyed us very much."

For most of World War II, the Curie family stayed in occupied France. Then Irène was forced to go back to a sanatorium in Switzerland, and Fred went into the underground. At the war's end, when General de Gaulle appointed Fred to head France's first Atomic Energy Commission, Irène served on the commission with him. Ultimately, as Marie had foreseen—and wished—Irène and then Fred served as head of the Curie.

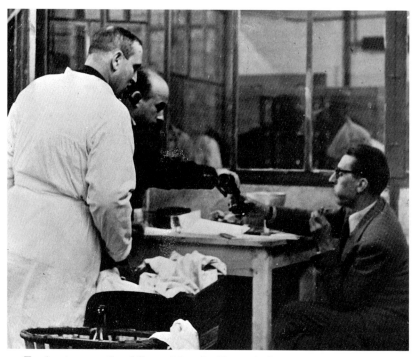

Fred eats a snack while waiting for France's first atomic pile to go active on December 1, 1948.

Irène in Warsaw in September 1948 at the World Congress of Intellectuals for Peace — an organization in which she was very active

December 25, 1955, was the first Christmas, except when Irène had been in sanatoriums, that Fred and Irène did not spend together in the Alps. He was not well enough to accompany her. Irène found it strange to be alone in their tiny chalet. "I regret, every day, that I have too much room for my personal belongings," she wrote him. "I am even sorry not to have to straighten up your bed, something, however, that I do not like to do. I miss you terribly."

This time Irène returned home without the usual benefits from a stay in the mountains. Leukemia finally claimed Irène at a premature 59, on March 17, 1956. Fred died on August 14, 1958, of liver problems caused by overexposure to polonium. Like Marie, Irène and Fred were victims of radiation research. Both were accorded state funerals.

Experiments from the Cooperative

KEEPING WATER HOT

Purpose: To determine if putting a cover on a pot of boiling water will keep the water hot longer.

Procedure:
1. Put an equal amount of water into two identical pans.
2. Heat the water in each pan to boiling.
3. Turn off the heat and put a candy thermometer into each pan.
4. Cover one pan and leave the other uncovered.
5. Record the temperature of the water every two minutes as the water cools. What do you notice?

Explanation: Evaporation of the water is taking place in both the covered and the uncovered pans. Evaporation causes the water in the pan to cool. You can feel the cooling effects of evaporation by wetting your hand and then blowing on it. Evaporation of sweat is how the human body cools itself.

In the uncovered pan, the water is evaporating into the room. In the covered pan, the water is evaporating, but as the evaporated water hits the cover, it condenses back into liquid water. Condensing is the opposite of evaporating. The water in the covered pan would cool much more slowly than the water in the uncovered pan.

—by Lois Fruen

THE LAW OF FALLING BODIES

Purpose: To test the law of falling bodies by describing a parabola.

Procedure:

1. Cover a board—at least two meters (6.5 feet) long—with paper.
2. Prop one end of the board up on two bricks. Mark a starting line at the top of the board.

3. Dip one side of a marble in washable ink.
4. Placing the marble at the starting line, allow the marble to roll down the inclined board. Measure the time it takes for the marble to make two marks on the paper covering the board.
5. Repeat the experiment measuring the time it takes for the marble to make four marks on the board, then six marks and eight marks.
6. Graph the results using the graph below. Note the parabola that is formed because of the acceleration caused by gravity.

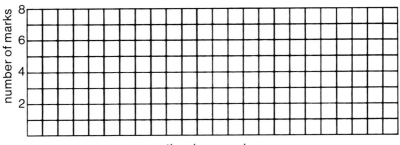

time in seconds

Explanation: The longer a falling body—the marble—falls, the faster it travels. This is called acceleration. The acceleration of a falling body is the same for each second of time. There are no spurts in its "pickup"—its fall is described as uniformly accelerated motion. Gravity acting on a falling body increases the speed of its fall by the same amount of speed that the body had during its first second of fall. The parabola shows how the speed of the fall increases uniformly.

—by Lois Fruen and Bruce Davis

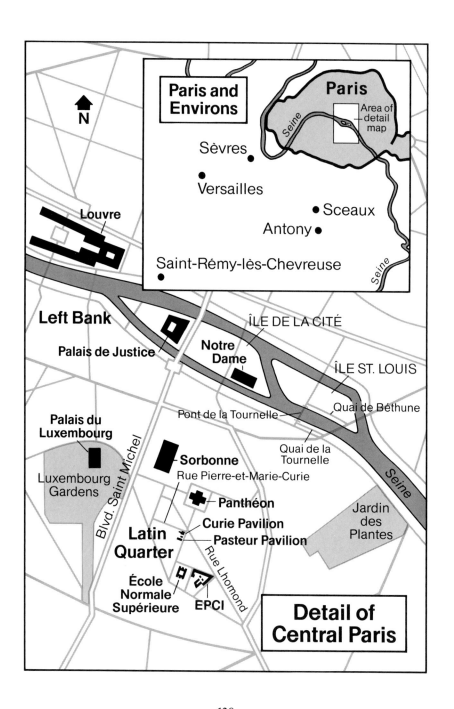

Sources

Quotes of less than six words have not been identified, except in cases where their sources are vital.

p.24 Marie Curie, *Pierre Curie* (New York: Macmillan, 1924), 171.

p.32 Archives Curie, Départment des Manuscrits, Bibliothèque Nationale, Paris.

p.32 Ibid.

p.37 M. Howorth, *Pioneer Research on the Atom* (New World Publishers, 1958), 22n.

p.40 Ève Curie, *Madame Curie*, trans. Vincent Sheean (New York: Doubleday, Doran & Co., 1937), 163.

p.42 Marie Curie, *Pierre Curie*, 169.

p.45 Ibid., 104.

p.53 Eugénie Feytis Cotton et Angèle Pompei, "Irène Joliot-Curie telle que l'ont connue E. Cotton et A. Pompei" (Projet d'un livre sur Irène Joliot-Curie, Laboratoire Curie, Institut du Radium, Paris), 2.

p.53 Archives Curie.

p.57 Cotton et Pompei, "Irène Joliot-Curie," 15.

p.60 Ève Curie, *Madame Curie*, 246.

p.61 Ibid., 248-9.

p.64 Cotton et Pompei, "Irène Joliot-Curie," 20.

p.68 R. McKown, *Irène Joliot-Curie* (Mesmer, 1962), 32.

p.69 Laboratoire Curie, Institut du Radium, Paris.

p.70 Ibid.

p.72 David Wilson, *Rutherford* (Cambridge: MIT Press, 1984).

p.74 Gillette Ziegler, ed., *Choix de Lettres de Marie Curie et Irène Joliot-Curie* (Paris: Les Éditeurs Français Réunis, 1974).

p.75 *Annales de l'Université de Paris*, 37:32.

p.75 Ève Curie, *Madame Curie*, 284.

p.77 Ziegler, *Lettres*.

p.79 Ibid.

p.79 Ibid.

p.85 Irène Joliot-Curie, "Marie Curie, Ma Mère," *Europe* 108 (1954): 103.

p.96 Robert W. Reid, *Marie Curie* (London: Collins, 1974), 268.

p.103 Emélie Roederer Joliot diary, Laboratoire Curie.

p.106 McKown, *Irène Joliot-Curie*, 72.

p.107 *Le Quotidien*, 31 March 1925.

p.109 Laboratoire Curie.

p.109 Ibid.

p.111 F. Giroud, *Une Femme Honorable* (Paris: Fayard, 1981), 365.

p.112 Ibid., 365.

p.115 Richard Rhodes, *The Making of the Atom Bomb* (New York: Simon and Schuster, 1986), 162.

p.115 Ibid., 404.

p.116 Spencer R. Weart, *Scientists in Power* (Cambridge: Harvard University Press, 1979), 44 [paraphrase].

p.117 Albert Laborde, Lecture on the 50th anniversary of the death of Pierre Curie, Laboratoire Curie.

p.117 S. Reidman, *Men and Women Behind the Atom* (Glasgow: Abelard-Schumann, 1958), 144.

p.118 M. Goldsmith, *Frederick Joliot-Curie* (London: Lawrence and Wishart, 1976), 42.

p.121 P. Biquard, *Frédéric Joliot-Curie* (Paris: Éd. Seghers, 1961).

p.129 Curie Archives, Rare Book and Manuscript Library, Columbia University, New York.

p.131 Lew Kowarski, oral interview by Charles Weiner, American Institute of Physics, New York.

p.134 Curie Archives, Rare Book and Manuscript Library, Columbia University, New York.

p.135 Laboratoire Curie.

Selected Bibliography

Books

Association Frédéric et Irène Joliot-Curie. *Souvenirs et Documents*. 1968.

Biquard, P. *Frédéric Joliot-Curie*. Paris: Éd. Seghers, 1961.

_____. *Langevin*. Paris: Éd. Seghers, 1969.

Chaskolskaia, Marianne. *Joliot-Curie*. Translated by G. Smirnov into French. Moscow: Éd. Mir, 1968.

Concasty, M. Louise. *Pierre and Marie Curie*. Paris: Bibliothèque Nationale, 1967.

Cotton, Eugénie Feytis. *Les Curies*. Paris: Éd. Seghers, 1963.

Crease, R.P., and C.C. Mann. *The 2nd Creation — Makers of a Revolution in 20th Century Physics*. New York: Macmillan, 1986.

Curie, Ève. *Madame Curie*. Translated by Vincent Sheean. New York: Doubleday, Doran & Co., 1937.

Curie, Marie. *Pierre Curie*. New York: Macmillan, 1924.

Destouches, C. *La Lumière Bleue*. Les Éditions du Temps, 1959.

Giroud, F. *Une Femme Honorable*. Paris: Fayard, 1981.

Goldschmidt, B. *L'Aventure Atomique*. Paris: Fayard, 1962.

Goldsmith, M. *The Curie Family*. Manchester: Heron Books, 1971.

_____. *Frederick Joliot-Curie*. London: Lawrence and Wishart, 1976.

Hoffman, B., and H. Dukas. *Einstein*. Paris: Éd. Seuil, 1975.

Howorth, M. *Pioneer Research on the Atom*. New World Publishers, 1958.

Kedrov, Fedor B. *Irène and Frédéric Joliot-Curie* (in Russian). 1973.

Langevin, André. *Paul Langevin*. Paris: Les Éditeurs Français Réunis, 1971.

Lot, F. *J. Perrin*. Paris: Éd. Seghers, 1963.

Marbo, Camille. *Souvenirs et Rencontres*. Paris: Éd. Grasset, 1968.

McKown, R. *Irène Joliot-Curie*. Mesmer, 1962.

Pflaum, Rosalynd. *Grand Obsession: Madame Curie and Her World*. New York: Doubleday, 1989.

Radvanyi, Pierre, and Monique Bordry. *La Radioactivité Artificielle*. Paris: Éd. Seuil, 1984.

Régaud, C. *Marie Curie*. Paris: Fondation Curie, 1934.

Reid, Robert W. *Marie Curie*. London: Collins, 1974.

Reidman, S. *Men and Women Behind the Atom*. Glasgow: Abelard-Schumann, 1958.

Rhodes, Richard. *The Making of the Atom Bomb*. New York: Simon and Schuster, 1986.

Romer, A., ed. *Discovery of Radioactivity and Transmutation*. New York: Dover, 1964.

Weart, Spencer R. *Scientists in Power*. Cambridge: Harvard University Press, 1979.

Wilson, David. *Rutherford*. Cambridge: MIT Press, 1984.

Ziegler, Gillette, ed. *Choix de Lettres de Marie Curie et Irène Joliot-Curie*. Paris: Les Éditeurs Français Réunis, 1974.

Articles

Biquard, Pierre. "Mon Ami, Joliot." *Pensée* 87 (Sep-Oct 1959).

Chadwick, Sir James. "Irène Curie." *Nature* 177 (26 May 1956).

Cotton, Eugénie Feytis. "J'ai connu Pierre Curie." *Horizons* 59 (April 1956).

_____. "Irène Curie-Joliot." *Pensée* 67 (1956).

_____. "Souvenirs." *Pensée* 87 (Sep-Oct 1959).

Curie, Ève. "Irène." *Marianne* (1936).

Joliot-Curie, Frédéric. "L'Énergie Atomique." *Atomes* 1 (Mar 1946).

_____. "La Première Pile Atomique Française." *Atomes* 35 (Feb 1949).

Joliot-Curie, Frédéric, et Irène Joliot-Curie. "Pierre Curie." *Pensée* (May-Jun 1956).

Joliot-Curie, Irène. "Marie Curie, Ma Mère." *Europe* 108 (1954).

Langevin, Hélène Joliot. "Gentner à Paris." CERN Publications.

Langevin, Paul. "Pierre Curie." *La Révue du Mois* (1906).

Manuscript Sources

American Institute of Physics, New York. Oral History interview of L. Kowarski by Charles Weiner.

Bibliothèque Nationale, Paris. Départment des Manuscrits. Curie Archives.

Columbia University, New York. Rare Book and Manuscript Library. Marie Curie Papers.

Laboratoire Curie, Institut du Radium, Paris.

   Material in files, including:

   Unpublished journals of Irène Joliot-Curie (circa 1900-1955) and Emélie Roederer Joliot.

   Press clippings.

   Unpublished manuscripts and speeches by: Eugénie Feytis Cotton and Angèle Pompei, Irène Joliot-Curie, Jeanne Laberrigue, André Langevin, Francis Perrin, P. Radvanyi.

   Correspondence between: Irène and Marie Curie; Irène and Frédéric Joliot-Curie; Paul Langevin and Frédéric Joliot-Curie; Paul Langevin and Irène Joliot-Curie; Missy Meloney, Irène Curie, and Marie Curie.

Interviews

Interviews by the author of numerous family members and colleagues of the Curies and Joliots, including:

   Pierre Joliot, Hélène Langevin-Joliot, Ève Curie (Mme Labouisse), Jean Langevin, Francis Perrin, Aline Lapique-Perrin, Dr. Raymond Latarjet, currently the Honorary Director of the Institut du Radium, and Dr. Bertrand Goldschmidt, the last researcher to have been selected by Marie Curie and a French pioneer of nuclear science.

Index

Perrin, Jean, 60, 66, 79, 119
piezo-quartz electrometer, 36, 99
polonium, 37-38, 40, 99, 106, 113,
115, 122

radioactivity, 36, 43, 54-55, 71, 113,
123
radioelements, 36, 71, 123
radium, 38, 40, 43-44, 45, 49-51, 81,
90-92, 93-96, 112, 129
use in medicine, 50, 77, 91-94,
97, 98
Radium, Institut du. *See* Curie
Institute
radon gas, 47, 49, 50, 91
Röntgen, Wilhelm, 33
Rutherford, Ernest, 71-72, 89, 115

Saint-Rémy-lès-Chevreuse, France,
58, 59
Sceaux, France, 29, 60, 62, 65-66,
73, 132
School for the Encouragement of
National Industry. *See* EPCI
Sèvres, 46-47, 50, 52, 65
sèvriennes, 46-47, 52-53, 55, 57,
65
shed on the rue Lhomond, 30,
41-43, 48

Sklodowska, Bronislawa (mother of
Manya), 10-12
Sklodowska, Bronya. *See* Dluski,
Bronya
Sklodowska, Hela. *See* Szalay, Hela
Sklodowska, Manya. *See* Curie,
Marie
Sklodowska, Zosia, 10-12
Sklodowski, Jozio, 10-12, 17, 100
Sklodowski, Vladislav, 8, 10-12, 17,
24, 32, 51
Solvay conferences, 70-72, 118-121
Sorbonne, 17, 24, 45, 55, 57, 61, 65,
66, 73, 81, 84-86, 89, 106-107
Szalay, Hania, 64, 69
Szalay, Hela, 8, 10-12, 64, 69, 100

thorium, 36

uranium, 34-37, 40-41

Warsaw, Poland, 10-14, 17, 24, 76,
112, 135
World War I, 78-86
World War II, 134

X rays, 33, 80, 82-87

Zorawski family, 14-17